Courting A
Woman's Soul

JOHN LEE

Mandala Publishing
Woodstock, Georgia

Published by Mandala Publishing, Woodstock, Georgia, a division of JL Creative Services, Inc.

Printed in the United States of America

Lee, John H.

Courting A Woman's Soul / John Lee. — 1st Ed.

ISBN 0-9746134-0-1

Dedicated to

DR. JAMES J. MAYNARD

Chapter 1

THE INTROVERT

"I have heard this music before, saith the body."
Mary Oliver

"How long has it been since you've had a real vacation?" Bill Stott, one of my best friends, asked. I had recently broken up with my latest soulmate. I was desperate and willing to try anything that would help me forget her.

"I took a few days off in London last year, and I stayed for three extra days in Sydney."

He frowned. "Not the same thing. You need to go someplace where no one knows you, and you can't hide behind your work. You've been stuck in a comfortable rut for too long. Better to be lonely in a new place."

I had heard that the definition of insanity was doing the same thing repeatedly and expecting different results. It was time to do something different. I called my travel agent and asked her to find a place where I could go and have some of this strange stuff people call "fun." After a short pause, she asked, "Where do you want to go?"

"Someplace where there aren't a lot of people."

"Then you might as well stay home," she laughed. She thought a moment and then said, "I have the perfect place for you. Trust me."

Growing up the way I did, with an Archie Bunker father and a Joan of Arc mother, I felt more comfortable outdoors than around people. I hung out in the woods with the rocks and trees and stared at drifting clouds that served as my own personal Rorschach. By age seven I had solitude down to an art. Sure, I was depressed most of the time, but at least it was familiar.

As a kid, I never felt like I belonged or fit in. I wasn't a no-neck jock, though my dad wanted me to be because I was big for my age and he hadn't been. I was neither brainy nor cool, but I had mastered the look that said, "Don't mess with me, because if you do I might cry all over you."

By my twenties, I wore my hair like a well-coifed hippie. I was vain enough to wash it every day and even occasionally blow it dry, trying to straighten my hair that always recurled in the Alabama humidity. I drank a lot and was introduced to pot in the mid-Seventies (the Sixties hit Alabama a decade late). I was an off-the-scale introvert. The only time I tolerated the company of other people was if I was drunk, stoned, or teaching college students, which often feels as surreal as the first two.

By the time I gave my travel agent carte blanche to plan my vacation, I had been a writer for nearly twenty years. I had reached a point in my career when I knew it was not necessary to drink alcohol, in spite of all the romantic notions about writers. I was semi-celibate, believing I could better give birth to my masterpiece if I wasn't getting laid. I was still in therapy every week trying to get a handle on what I really wanted to be when I grew up—a cowboy, policeman, Indian chief, or an honest-to-God really good writer who just didn't know what to write. I gave talks about the books I'd written and occasional readings at conferences and bookstores. I had several good friends that I saw regularly, but most of my romantic relationships didn't last as long as the flu. Sometimes people asked me to dinner after lectures but I usually declined. "Thank you very much, but I'm exhausted. I think I'll just go back to my hotel," was my standard response. What they didn't know was I was scared to death to be with a small group of strangers, though one-on-one was not too bad.

And where did my travel agent book me? Club Med in the Turks & Caicos Islands, about 100 miles south of Miami and a stone's throw from Cuba. I had heard of Club Med since the Seventies. It was *the* place to get high, drunk, and laid. Even Quasimodo could accomplish all three in less than a week. (It turns out that although some Club Meds are still wild, many have become more family-oriented. But I didn't know that then.) Just the thought of vacationing at Club Med terrified me, but I had to take the chance. I needed this vacation.

CHAPTER 2

THE VACATION

"Some people claim that there's a woman to blame,
But I know, it's my own damn fault."
Jimmy Buffet

On a scorching July morning, I flew from Austin to Miami to make connections to Providenciales. In the Miami airport, the flight board clearly stated I should go to Gate 10, but I went to Gate 3 instead. There were no waiting passengers or agents at this gate, but for reasons I still do not understand, I sat there for over thirty minutes. Then, over the loudspeaker, I heard the announcement: "Final call for flight 777 to Providenciales leaving at Gate 10." I was seven gates away. I ran as hard as my middle-aged body would go and made it inside just before they closed the door. Ironically, the plane taking me on vacation would have been the first flight I had ever missed.

When I got off the plane, I ran into a small group heading to Club Med. We were told that our shuttle to the club was delayed and we would have to wait. Lana, a beautiful nurse from San Diego, was the first to introduce herself. I was sure she was my one-way ticket to paradise: a tanned, blonde Californian in the helping profession, and if anybody needed help, I did. As soon as she said hello, Hans, a short Austrian man, stuck out his hand and aimed it clearly at Lana. After their eyes locked and held for a moment, he turned to me and introduced himself. He was a jeweler and traveled quite extensively. Although he was married, this was his fourth trip to Club Med. Those damn lucky Europeans and their complete lack of morals, I thought. God, how I envy them.

After we all said where we were from and got pleasantries out of the way, a slim, very blonde, white-toothed Italian woman came over. "Hello, my name is Isabella, but my English is no very good. Is this place where we caught the bus?" As luck would have it, Hans spoke fluent Italian and had an almost supernatural way of making deep eye contact with females. Any idea of my being with either of these women was going quickly from slim to none. Clearly Hans, with his golden necklace and his silver tongue that could speak five different languages, was going to have a very good time.

Finally the van arrived and we all loaded in. I sat up front with the driver who spoke limited English. Hans sat in between Lana and Isabella with a big-assed grin on his face. It was after ten that night when we arrived at the Club. The staff greeted us with loud Caribbean music, flowers and some kind of sweet, punchy rum drink. Declining the initiatory island libation, I went to the pool where there was a weak Dionysian attempt to entertain the guests with people dancing and carrying lit torches. One of the women was supposed to be a virgin being offered to the god of the sea or something. I watched for a few minutes, bored and disgusted, then went straight to bed. If this is what the rest of the vacation would be like, then vacations were highly overrated, and I'd seen enough of Club Med.

The next morning I awoke with the same sense of displeasure I've greeted the morning with for years. All of this manufactured fun wasn't going to work, and would probably turn my stomach. But when I walked out of my room, the sultry Caribbean air wrapped me with an intoxicating sensuality that banished my fears.

I found the main dining hall where every kind of breakfast known to man was served. The poached salmon, eggs benedict, and sushi looked great. The chef must have seen me coming, because there were ample portions of scrambled eggs and grits. Lana, Hans, and Isabella walked in as soon as I sat down. It seemed we would form an unlikely tourist quartet. I'm not sure how or why I gravitated to these people, but I latched on to them for dear life.

Hans, in his excellent English and beautiful Italian, tried to coordinate the conversation so we could all understand each other. Lana spoke fluent Southern Californian and I spoke Southern Appalachian, so we needed a translator only a few times that week.

We all made a conscious decision to do things together and started planning our day. I went to the bulletin board to see what the tour guide suggested for the day.

While I stood at the bulletin board, I saw a woman so hot she could thaw an iceberg. My God, she was gorgeous. She had blonde, shoulder-length hair, and her legs were made of the finest porcelain. As she came out of the ocean and strode closer, I noticed there was a significant age difference between us. I guessed her to be twenty at best and jail bait at worst, but I still couldn't take my eyes off her. Her blue-green eyes had a maturity and certitude about them. If I were twenty years younger, I would do whatever it took to get her to spend the rest of her life with me.

I felt like a dirty old man. I needed to jump in the sea and take a salty bath.

She stopped in front of me and smiled. "If you're looking for something to do besides getting sunburned, you should try the full-day excursion," she said, pointing to the bulletin board. "I went yesterday and it was fantastic. We snorkeled, had a delicious picnic on a deserted beach, hand-fed iguanas, and toured ancient Indian caves. And to top it all off, the guide is hilarious."

I introduced myself and thanked her for the advice.

"My name is Susan," she said.

I stuck out my hand to shake hers and she looked me in the eye. "I have a boyfriend back in Miami. We broke up a few days before this trip. He got mad and canceled, so I decided to come alone, relax and get some sun. Then two days before I left we got back together. I'm telling you so you'll know I'm not looking for romance."

I gazed at her and took a deep breath, knowing way down inside that I'm pretty shallow and not nearly as conscientious as I would like people to think. It took me a few moments, but I finally found some sincere place floating around in the soles of my feet and said, "That's fine. I just got out of a relationship. I came to relax and have some fun, too."

She cocked her head to one side and grinned. "You need to go on the excursion. When you get back, we'll compare notes."

I went back to the dining hall and told the others about the beautiful young woman and her suggestion. We all agreed to cough up the hundred dollars each. I didn't know it then, but Mr. Serious was about to have the most fun of his entire adult life.

Susan was right. Ron, our guide and driver, was as hilarious as he was huge. He had hands the size of boat oars and a head as bald as Kojak's. While we bounced over the blue-green water, he used the boat as his stage and had us rolling with laughter.

Our first stop was at an aboriginal cave. They were cool, wet, and very slippery, but quite fascinating. He guided us through the rocky labyrinth with the ease of someone who had lived around those ancient passages all his life. But his familiarity with the terrain did not deter his enthusiasm about their grandeur and history.

I had seen many caves in the Southern Appalachians where I grew up, but these caves were otherworldly. They were part of an island that two weeks before I had never heard of, and I was experiencing them with people I hardly knew. I especially enjoyed helping Isabella over the slippery rocks before old slippery Hans could get to her.

After touring the caves, we traveled to what divers consider one of the world's most beautiful reefs. I had never snorkeled before. I had never wanted to. Perhaps it was due to the way my father taught me how to swim, by throwing me off a twelve-foot pier when I was six. I had never thought of swimming, skin diving, or snorkeling as something to look forward to. Swimming was for survival, not pleasure.

The color of the water changed many times on our boat trip. Sometimes it was turqoise, other times light green, and, in the deepest areas, it was a sparkling pure blue. It was much more inviting than the murky Tennessee River, where I nearly drowned before my dad jumped in to rescue me.

I took a deep breath and looked at the unfamiliar world I was about to plunge into. Open water terrified me, but this crystal green liquid with washes of turquoise seemed an entryway to paradise. There was movement beneath the surface—pinks and reds and flashes of silver that signaled life.

Ron gave us five minutes of instruction and handed me a jar of Vaseline. He explained that if I smeared it on my mustache and beard, my mask would stay on better. "All you have to do is float with your face two inches in the water and watch," he said. He should have said, *For those who have never done this, your whole conception of life is about to change.*

I clumsily adjusted the mask over my face and placed the snorkel in my mouth. They felt so foreign. Then I lowered myself into the water and suddenly everything became easy and natural. I was part of a world teeming with color and life. An orange clownfish darted by a coral outcropping with more colors than Van Gogh's palette. Aquatic life swayed to the rhythm of the ocean's gentle current. Luminous corals stretched their ancient fingers towards me. I was like a kid again in the truest sense, before father, mother, and rickety wooden piers. I was a gray-haired newborn.

I could have snorkeled all day. All I had to do was lie down, float with my face in the water, and be moved to tears by the beautiful landscape. I was thankful for all the miracles that led to this moment.

Exhausted, but exhilarated, the five of us climbed back into the boat, and Ron sped us away to a deserted sand dune where we had wine, champagne, and sandwiches. After touring the little island, we took a nap beneath palm trees before heading off to Iguana Island.

Ron slid the boat onto shore as smoothly as a baby rests its head on its mother's shoulder. Hundreds of iguanas of all sizes came running towards the boat. "They have seen white people before, and to my knowledge have eaten only one or two," smiled Ron as he distributed bits of bread leftover from lunch. "Here you can feed them. They'll take it right out of your hand." And they did. Some were a little shyer than others and we had to throw them the bread. I decided to walk further into the bushes and see if I could find their introverted kin.

Sure enough, there were hundreds more hiding in the bushes. They scattered as I approached. I could barely see them, yet there were as many of them as there were taking the bread out of my friends's hands. I noticed the extroverts were fat and happy, which made me think of Hans, who wasn't exactly fat, but full of self-confidence, and happier than any of us. (He was also the only one cheating on a spouse.) I felt like one of the underfed iguanas hiding in the bushes.

After we fed the iguanas, we headed back to the club. Just as the sun was setting, we neared shore and saw JoJo, the Lone Dolphin, so called because he swam those waters by himself and had been doing so for twelve years. Another loner I could relate to. He jumped into the air, executed a half spin, and swam alongside the boat until we docked. Perfect.

It was the most fun day of my adult life, even without sex. I didn't think anything could top it.

CHAPTER 3
THE BEGINNING OF A FRIENDSHIP

*"I think this is the beginning of a
beautiful friendship."*
Casablanca

That evening, after a long nap, I got dressed for dinner with the gang. I went a little early, hoping I'd see Susan. I couldn't wait to thank her for one of the greatest days of my life. As I approached the restaurant, I saw her coming towards me with an entourage of a dozen people. She wore a simple yellow cotton dress and very girlish sandals. (Most of the women I had dated were the Birkenstock type.) A mixture of men and women, young and old, they all wanted the time and attention from this woman whose smile was as big as Texas. If she weren't so young, I would have chased this unofficial Homecoming Queen of Club Med until I collapsed in the sand or into her alabaster arms.

"Hello," I said as she came alongside me. "Could I speak to you for a moment?"

Smiling at her friends, she excused herself politely, and we walked towards the beach.

"I won't keep you long, but there's something I want to tell you." I looked into her beautiful blue-green eyes and said, "I want to thank you from the bottom of my heart. Had you not appeared when you did, I'm sure I wouldn't have taken the excursion. I would have kept the gregarious genie in his little bottle and been satisfied to sit on the beach, read, and go home with a terrible sunburn. Then I could go home and say, 'See, I can take a vacation just like normal people.' Now I'm going to try everything this week from wind surfing to sailing to tennis lessons—and I'm going dancing every night." I felt a tear sliding down my cheek.

She took a deep breath. "Wow, I didn't know a little suggestion would make such a difference. You haven't had much fun lately, have you?"

I cringed. Was it that obvious? "You're right. For years, I have considered work to be my fun. I had no idea that something as simple as slipping a snorkel over my face could change the way I see the world. Hell, I haven't even been dancing since I stopped drinking ten years ago."

"Maybe you can save me a dance or two this week." She glanced over to my group of friends. "I think they're waiting for you," she said. "I'm glad you had such a great day. I have a feeling you're opening up to a lot of new things. Let's touch base as much as we can this week, okay?"

"See you later," I said, slightly embarrassed that I wept in front of a woman I hardly knew. But I figured, what the hell. She was just being nice to an old guy rambling about not having much fun. We probably wouldn't get a chance to say more than an occasional hello over the next few days.

Every day I watched for Susan to appear and at some point in the day or night, there she would be. By the third afternoon I found out she wasn't nearly as young as I thought. She would turn 30 on her next birthday. I didn't believe her until she showed me her driver's license. She graduated from college with a fine arts degree and was an artist with work on display in some of Miami's finest galleries. She was born in Ecuador; her mother was Colombian and her father was from Indiana. Her blonde hair, blue eyes, and light skin made every Anglo think she was a gringa, but her fluent Spanish convinced every Latino she spoke to that she wasn't.

Mostly I discovered that she and I had a lot in common. We both loved movies and books, and we both breathed air and drank water. We were made for each other.

During the first few days or even months of a possible romantic relationship, the head bounces up and down with dozens of "me, toos," like those little dogs people put on their dashboards. "I like coffee." "Wow, that's incredible—so do I." "You like the movies. This is just too much—I love the movies." And so it goes. As a matter of fact, a beautiful woman can even get a bubba like me to say "I love ballet" during the first six months. Although I knew there was no chance of romance, we got along great, and my head did a lot of bob-bing.

Each day we would get together and tell each other our dreams from the night before; sometimes we'd discuss our dreams about the future. She wanted to get married, have three children and paint. I wanted to get married, have two children and write. I kept thinking it was just too damn bad that she was involved with someone and all that could come of this was a friendship that wouldn't last a month once we were tucked safely back home.

With this in mind, I started looking for someone more romantically available. After all, I was at Club Med. Surely there was at least one woman who would walk the moonlit beach with me and watch the sun come up.

CHAPTER 4
PRIMAL VIEWS

"This is not Life. This is only a drill. If this had actually been Life, we would have been instructed where to go and what to do."
Unknown

There is an old saying down South: If it'd been a snake, it would have bit ya.

Hans, Isabella, Lana and I became inseparable. We dined, danced, water-skied and sailed together. Isabella and I grew more and more comfortable with each other, partly because Hans and Lana were practically living together — they slept together from the first night. They continued to meet us for meals and to hang out and endure the dopey shows the staff orchestrated in the evening, but by nine they were off doing something I had not done in a long time.

Isabella and I tried to talk but it became apparent that if we were going to communicate it would have to be by body language, facial expression, and gesture. I managed to learn that she was a doctor and lived in Milan, but most of the time her broken English and my non-existent Italian forced us to fall back on resources I hadn't used since I was a toddler. Somehow, this freed us up to be more childlike and reduced our anxiety. We didn't need words to have a great time. We danced, walked on the beach pointing at stars, laughed and played like kids. Without words, we managed to be ourselves.

But near the end of the week, Isabella began acting a bit cool towards me. For the life of me I couldn't figure out why. It couldn't have been something I said, because I hadn't said anything to her.

Hans came to the restaurant early that evening. We sat outside and watched the pink sun sink into the green sea. Lana and Isabella were still getting dressed.

"Hans, I need to ask your advice on a delicate matter. You speak Italian. Has Isabella said something to you that might lead you to believe I have offended her in some way?"

"No, she has not said anything, but I can tell you she is very attracted to you. Why have you not taken her to your bed yet?'

"Because we don't know each other that well. Besides, she just seems to want companionship. She calls Italy every day, checking to see if her ex-boyfriend called her. When she comes back from the calls she looks heartbroken, so I try to take her mind off of him. We have a great time just being together."

"You American men make me laugh. Here you are with this beautiful woman who is very attracted to you, and you spend all day together while Lana and I make love. My guess is that Isabella is angry because she thinks you don't find her attractive and you only want her for a dance partner."

"How do you know this? Has she said something to you?"

"She doesn't have to say anything. I can see it in her eyes when she looks at you. You could too if you weren't so naïve or so American – or so often looking for that young blonde girl we see you talking to every day."

I could not believe how bold he was. He challenged my enlightened, civilized view of women and everything the feminist revolution stood for.

"Isabella is a European woman. Most European women know their men have mistresses or other lovers, and now many European women feel they can do the same. Isabella doesn't care any less for her old boyfriend just because she is attracted to you. She is not an American woman who delights in being courted for weeks before making love. My friend, I must tell you that many of you American men make a lot of trouble for yourselves by not understanding one essential thing—American women, just like European women, just like every woman I've ever known, wants a man to take them. They do not want you to ask for their permission. They want their man to take the initiative and take them. Don't misunderstand, they don't want rough and tough, they just want direct."

I couldn't believe what he was telling me. It was so politically incorrect, and yet just the night before as we lay in a hammock looking at the night sky and the dark water, I had asked Isabella if she wanted to go to my room and make love.

When I told Hans this he laughed. "Of course she said no. She's supposed to say no. Even Lana would have said no if I had asked. Women have their pride and dignity. Neither of these beautiful women are prostitutes. They have to say no. However, unlike you, my dear American friend, I didn't ask Lana if she wanted to—how would you Americans say it?—'take it to the next level.' I took her to my bedroom and told her she was the most beautiful woman I'd ever seen and I started making love to her. I can't speak for all women, perhaps many American women want to be asked, but perhaps many do not. So my guess is that because you asked her, Isabella feels you don't really want her, and she feels rejected and angry."

I was angry myself. I suspected some of what he said was probably true, but I didn't know which part. I wanted to say, "Oh great European Love God, tell me what to do." Before I could say anything he said, "Let me tell you what to do. If you are attracted to Isabella, then take her to your room and make love to her."

I sat in my white, plastic pool chair and felt like an idiot. Was he right? It went against everything I'd struggled to learn in the last twenty-five years. Did women still have a primitive urge to be taken? I know most men are still packing that urge to do so, but most of us have become so nice we don't talk about it—or act on it.

Truth is, a great confusion has fallen over America like a dark cloud. American men don't know whether to open a car door for a woman, pull out her chair at dinner, or what. Women aren't sure what is expected of them, either. Do I sleep with him on the third date or will he think I'm too easy? Should I pick up the check occasionally or will he think I'm too aggressive? Should I ask him out or follow "The Rules" and never call him, never pick up a check, not make love until he proposes?

I saw a lot of books being read that week by the pool and on the beach, and none of them was The Rules, but nearly every woman I knew had read it, even if they disagreed with it. The Rules suggested we all pretend it was still 1950, Ike was in the White House, and it was Happy Days for everyone.

Now Hans appears and says, it's not the Fifties, it's not even the Twenty-first century. It's the way it's always been and the way it always will be— man takes woman, woman feigns resistance but actually wants to be taken. While John Grey is making millions telling people that men are from

Mars and women are from Venus, Hans is saying when it comes to love, romance and sex, we are all from the same horny planet—where men take women to bed and women like it—and both deal with the acrimony or alimony later.

I probably offended several readers by saying all this. But keep in mind, I'm only repeating what Hans told me. I don't know what the hell men and women want. Like everybody else, I'm just trying to figure it out as I go along.

I didn't know whether Hans was right, but his obvious happiness, and Lana's, gave me something to think about.

Lana joined us on the deck, moonfaced from all the fun she and Hans were having together. Hans left to buy cigarettes. I turned to Lana, smiled, and said, "You look radiant tonight."

"Thanks. Isn't this place really cool?"

"You mean, 'Isn't Hans the greatest,' don't you?"

She smiled an even larger smile, exposing several thousand dollars' worth of perfectly straight teeth. "Yeah, well that too. He is pretty wonderful. I sure wish he wasn't married. But I'm on vacation, and he's a great guy."

"Let me ask you something, if it's not being too personal."

"Okay."

"You know Hans is married. You know you're an attractive woman who could have her pick of men, right? And yet, you've chosen Hans. Why?"

She looked up in the sky and watched the seagulls circling overhead.

"All I can say is I've never met a man who knows so clearly what he wants. He was so direct about his desire for me. He came right out on the first night and said, 'I want to make love to you.'"

Now, don't get the wrong impression of Lana. We talked a great deal that week and she was no slut. Normally she would wait, hold back, and be good. She had as bad a track record with men as I did with women. This was her first time to try a vacation at anything like a Club Med.

"It's just that most of the men back home don't really know what they want. If they do, then they always come at you sideways and still end up unable to make a commitment. Hans said he was married and that he wanted me. His honesty was refreshing, and it turned me on. I like a man who goes after what he wants and isn't afraid to be told no."

"So," I took a deep breath, "he just took you, is that right?"

"Yeah, I'd have to say that's exactly what he did. But it's not as if I didn't have free will, or I had forgotten everything I'd learned over the years, but I'm tired of all the fucking games. Men don't know what they want; women don't know what they want or what men want. I just want to be with someone who knows what he wants—even if it isn't moral or decent."

"Thanks for your honesty. I'm sad to admit I've been one of those guys flying around women like those seagulls up there."

"I know," she said. "I've been watching the way Isabella looks at you and you haven't done a thing. She really wants you. But don't think we haven't seen you eyeballing that young woman. I bet you haven't made a move on her, either."

"Well, in my defense Susan is too young. Besides, she made it clear from the start that she's got a boyfriend back in Miami, and she just wants to be friends. I have to respect that. As for Isabella, I really don't see what you and Hans see. I figured she was attracted to Hans, but you just got there first, so she was settling for someone to keep her company while she pined over her old boyfriend."

"Well, you're wrong. I can't speak for Susan, but trust me, I can tell when a woman is attracted to a man, and Isabella is very attracted to you."

Isabella walked out of the dining room with Hans. His arm was wrapped around her, and they were both chattering at the same time. And smiling.

I smiled, too.

CHAPTER 5

THE DREAM

"When I want you in the night
When I want you to hold me tight
Whenever I want you all I have to do
Is dream, dream, dream, dream…"
The Everly Brothers

It was the last night of my vacation, and I was still thinking long and hard about what Hans and Lana said. I hadn't taken a step toward bringing Isabella to bed. If I was going to do it, this was the night.

Earlier that day Isabella and I went for a swim together in the ocean. We splashed around playfully and had a mock fight. She wrapped her athletic legs around my back, and I swung her around and around. Like most European women on the island, she took off her top to sunbathe and swim. She pressed her firm breasts against me. We kissed long, deep, and hard.

We got out of the water and lay on the beach for a couple of hours. Finally, Isabella announced she'd had enough sun and was going to her room to take a nap, shower, and change. She said she would meet us all for dinner around nine. I said, "Could we make it eight? Remember, I'm not from Europe." She laughed, "Fine, eight for our last night together."

I planned how I would "take" Isabella before it was too late. I had one more opportunity, and after the erotic swim we had earlier that day, I felt more than ready. Somehow, I also had to figure out a way to see Susan either that night or in the morning, given I would be leaving at noon the next day. I could not figure out how to accomplish both.

As I was heading to my room, I saw Susan sitting by the pool. This was the first time that a half dozen people were not milling around her.

"How are you doing?" I said.

"Pretty good. How are you?"

"Well, I'm a little sad. I have to leave Paradise tomorrow. I guess we won't have much time to talk before I go."

"What are you doing tonight?"

"I'm going to meet the gang for dinner and then see a few minutes of the show and turn in early." I was lying, but what could I say? I'm going to eat dinner and have another woman for dessert?

"How about I save you a seat at the show tonight?" she offered.

"Yeah, that would be great. Could you save four seats?"

"Sure, no problem."

For half a minute, I thought she meant she was going to save me a seat next to her so we could be together. So I decided to make a fool of myself, after all, it wouldn't be the first time and it was the last night. I said, "Will the seats be by you?"

"I hope so. I want to talk to you before you leave."

I went to my room and took a nap. I dreamt that Susan I and were walking alone on the beach. I kissed her and told her she shouldn't go back to the guy in Miami — she should come to Austin and be with me.

When I awoke, I felt sad. Here I was fantasizing about Susan while planning to make love to Isabella later in the evening. I got dressed, put on cologne, something I hadn't done in years, and walked to the restaurant. It was eight, and Hans and Lana were waiting by the pool. We all felt the strain on our collective psyche since it was our last night together. Hans would stay a week longer and so would Isabella. Lana and I would leave at the same time tomorrow.

We started talking about the week we had. I went to the bulletin board where the official photographer posted pictures he'd taken that week. There were several photos of Hans, Lana, Isabella and I together. I purchased four copies of the picture with the four of us together on the first night. There were also several pictures of Susan by herself, which I couldn't understand because every time I saw her she had a herd of people around her. I kept looking at Susan's picture. She was just standing there in that simple yellow sundress looking radiant. I requested a copy of her picture as well. I hid her picture in my journal, feeling like a dirty old man. I took the other packet of pictures back to the group and gave them each a copy. By this time, Isabella had arrived. When she saw the photographs, she started to cry. Lana held back a tear, and Hans asked how much he owed for the photographs. I said, "Nothing, it's my gift to you all."

We all did a group hug thing. Hans didn't hug too hard, but we all got the idea. We felt something special had happened between the four of us, and that it wasn't luck or an accident that we all came together when we did. I knew had it not been for their friendship and support, I would not have had nearly the fun that I did.

We went into the restaurant, and I tried everything they served. I knew it was the last time I'd be able to eat so much food with so little guilt. We laughed a lot and then went to watch a flying trapeze show put on by guests and their teachers. As soon as we got close to the theatre, I heard Susan's voice calling my name. Finally I saw her.

"Over here," she called from near the front. We walked through the crowd and I gave Susan a platonic hug. "I saved you the best seats in the house," she said. Sure enough, there were four empty chairs on the front row.

"Where are you sitting?"

"My friends and I are taking the second row so you four could have the best seats. It's your last night, after all."

I thanked her and said, "You and your friends should take the front row. We'll sit where you're sitting." This was code for, *I can't believe you're not sitting next to me, so take the damn seats and I'll forget the dream I had earlier this afternoon.*

"No, I insist. Please be my special guest this evening."

We all sat down and watched people flying through the air. During intermission, I said to Isabella, "Come with me. I want to take you for a last walk down the beach."

She looked at me a little funny. "Okay."

I told Lana and Hans that we would see them in the morning for breakfast. They both knew what I intended. I leaned over and told Susan I wanted to see her before breakfast in the morning, and could she be a little early so we could say goodbye? She agreed to meet me at eight, an hour before breakfast.

Isabella and I made our way to the beach hand in hand. We first went to the dock where the motorboats were tied. I had taken her skiing with me earlier that day at the same spot. I hadn't skied in twenty years but I loved it, even the part where I fell on my ass trying to slalom and swallowed half the ocean.

We started kissing at a feverish pace. I closed my eyes and pretended to love her, pretended she was my ex, pretended that I was just as European as Hans. Everything was pretend except for my longing. I said to Isabella, "Come with me, we're going to your room." She didn't hesitate a moment. When we got to the room, I picked her up, pushed the door open with my foot, and laid her on the bed. I looked into her eyes and knew she was ready. I'd been ready all week. I took off her blouse and kissed her wildly, as if she was the greatest love of my life. We kissed, explored, and caressed for over an hour.

I sought her eyes. Even in the dark I saw that she was crying. I held her gently, forgetting we were nude and needy. "Why are you crying?" I asked, bewildered.

"It is nothing. Make love to me."

"Please tell me why you are so sad before we go any further."

"My English is no good. You would not understand me. I am just being foolish girl. I don't want you to see little girl. I want you to make love to me."

"Okay, we'll make love, but we have all night. First tell me why you're crying. You've meant so much to me this week. I feel like we're good friends."

"That is why I cry. I feel we are friends and you really like me and respect me. I wish I could meet someone like you in Italy who could be my friend and lover. I think you are such a man. You would be honest and not like most Italian or European men who lie to their lovers and wives as if it is nothing. My father always kept a mistress. The man I was in love with was always with other women. But you, you are different from those men."

A mixture of passion and desperation seeped into her words. "I could fall in love with you if you come to Italy. Say you will come. You can write there. Milan is a beautiful city." She stopped and looked away. "But I know you will not come. No one has ever really loved me before. You would be the first to really love Isabella in the way I always dreamed. So I am sad."

I looked into her eyes and glimpsed a beautiful soul covered by sorrow.

I couldn't—I wouldn't—add to his woman's pain. After what she said, I knew she was not looking for a Club Med screwing. She wanted and needed to be loved, and it couldn't be by me. I held her close for a long time as she wept.

"We are not going to be lovers, are we?" she asked timidly.

"No, Isabella. You deserve the kind of love I can't give you, but I can be your friend. If we made love, I would be included on the list of men who have hurt you. I have hurt enough women in my life."

Why had it taken me four decades to realize the difference between lust and love? Lust takes everything and gives nothing; love gives everything and takes so very little.

"I will lie here all night if you like and hold you, but I can't make love to you. I guess I'm not European enough."

Her bottom lip quivered, and she tried to smile. "Would you hold me until I fall asleep? Then I think it would be better if you go."

I nodded and watched as she reached for a small teddy bear sitting on the couch. I wondered if this Italian doctor, so mature in every way, brought this toy with her, or if she bought it on the island. She clasped the teddy bear to her chest. "I hope you don't think Isabella a little girl."

"Not at all. You are a beautiful woman. Go to sleep. When you wake up we will all have breakfast and say goodbye. Maybe some day I will visit you in Italy. You can show me all the beautiful places in Milan. Good night, my beautiful Isabella."

After she fell asleep I walked back to my room, wondering if I'd done the right thing, or just the nice thing. I thought back on the times I had made love to other women, or they made love to me, when neither of us really wanted anything more than closeness or gentleness. I remember one time while I was living with Meg and I awoke from a terrible nightmare. I went downstairs where she was making breakfast. I looked at her and she could see I was upset.

"Honey, you look so sad." She put down what she was doing. "Would you like for me to hold you?"

I started weeping and said, "Yes, I had a horrible dream."

She sat down, leaned against the wall, and spread her legs wide, not in a sexual way, but in a way that said, *Come here.*

I allowed her to wrap herself around me and wept for over thirty minutes. This was the first time I had let a woman hold me without the feeling that something was expected of me. After I told Meg about the dream, I said, "Thank you for being there for me."

She said, "Thank you for asking for what you really needed. Not too long ago, you would have used lovemaking to try and soothe yourself. Then I would have felt like a mother making love to her child. It feels good to me, too, to be here for you in this way."

Many years ago, I wrote one of my first poems about that day.

ANCIENT PATHS

Geese know the ancient path
their parents laid out for them
in the sky.
When horses are born
the first thing they do is walk,
even if their legs are like water.
Animals seem to know what to do
when it's time.

I remember the first time
a woman said, "Let me hold you."
This was a path I could not remember.
I turned and twisted my body like a
colt leaving the birth canal.
Finally, I fell into the deep grass of
her arms.
I lay on my left arm
until it went sound asleep.
Unlike the newborn, I didn't care if I
ever
stood on my own two feet
again.

CHAPTER 6
THE LONG GOODBYE

"Sweet is the memory of distant friends!
Like the mellow rays of the departing sun,
it falls tenderly, yet sadly, on the heart."
Washington Irving

The last morning at Club Med I felt a mixture of grief and fear. I knew this was the last time I would see these wonderful people, and I would never have this experience again. I felt as if I had been frozen all my adult life and the tropical sun and camaraderie finally had thawed me out. But what really made me sad was knowing I would never see Susan again. I wanted to make our last meeting special, so I wrote a poem (a bad one) and looked around for something to give her for a present. There beside my bed lay my favorite book of poetry, Robert Bly's *Loving A Woman in Two Worlds*. I had been carrying it around for years. It was the perfect gift. It had a special poem in it that I planned to read to her that morning, "A Third Body." I got dressed, grabbed my journal and the book, and went to say goodbye.

I arrived at the pool a little early and reread my poem and Bly's beautiful poem. Just as I finished, Susan walked up to me.

She slid into one of the pool chairs and looked at the sunrise. "I'm sad. This is our last day."

"Susan, I have so much to say to you. Our daily talks have meant a lot to me. I wish you the best."

She reached out and squeezed my arm gently.

"I don't have much time before my friends arrive," I said. "I want to read you these two poems before they get here."

I read her my bad poem, which she politely said she liked very much. Then I read her Bly's poem. She started weeping before I could finish it.

"Both poems are wonderful. Robert Bly's poem takes my breath away. Thank you for these two gifts."

I pressed my fingers against the cover of Bly's book. "I've carried this book around with me for a long time. I want you to have it. I hope when you read it, you'll remember this place and time, and maybe even think of me."

"You make it sound like we're never going to see each other again," she said, taking the book and holding it to her heart. "We've become friends. I want us to stay in touch when we get back home. Let's exchange addresses and phone numbers right now." She started writing hers on a piece of paper and I wrote mine in the book I'd just given her thinking, *God she's nice to do this.* I wished she wasn't so beautiful or that I wasn't so damn old. I wished I was blind so I couldn't see what a great woman was sitting across from me and slipping away, a woman who was just being nice to an old man. I was certain she had passed her address around to every man, woman and child and said the same thing, *Let's keep in touch.*

"Look, I know when we leave we'll both go back to our separate lives," I said, "but if you'll write or call, I will, too. I promise."

"I promise, too," she said without a moment's hesitation.

We gave each other a warm hug that I wished would never end and said goodbye.

I walked slowly and sadly to the dining area, wishing goodbyes didn't have to be so painful.

I composed myself and ate breakfast with my friends. We also exchanged addresses. There were a few tears and a lot of promises that we'd all meet again next year and relive that which can only be lived once. With addresses safely tucked away, we all said goodbye. Isabella asked if she could walk me to the bus that would take us to the airport. When we arrived at the bus, all the staff had lined up to tell us goodbye and sing some kind of Caribbean leaving-the-island song. I was so preoccupied with Isabella I didn't hear a word of it. As we shook hands with the staff, I was surprised and moved by the fact that they all knew my name. Several were in tears as we hugged goodbye, especially my small, slender tennis instructor. She stepped out of the line and held my hand. "You made teaching more fun that I've had in a long time."

I couldn't believe my ears—I had made something "fun" for somebody I barely knew.

"You were hilarious, and once you relaxed, you got to be pretty good at tennis. We all had a better week because of you. Have a great trip home. We'll miss you."

After several others said their good-byes, I turned to Isabella and held her tightly, then kissed her like I would never kiss anyone again. The staff clapped, cheered, and whistled. I enjoyed it so much that I got off the bus and did it again just for the sheer fun of it. Under different circumstances, I could have spent many good days and nights with Isabella.

The long goodbye turned into five or six letters and several phone calls to Isabella. I even bought a tape to try and learn Italian. We had discussed the possibility of me visiting her during the Christmas holidays. This was in July. By September, we were both just fond memories.

Lana and I called each other a couple of times after we got back to the states. We reminisced and talked about Isabella and Hans. She thought about visiting during the holidays also and we talked about going to Europe together. She couldn't figure out how to pull it off without Hans' wife finding out. Turned out it didn't matter. In October she called and said Hans had written her a "Dear Jane" letter, saying he didn't think it would be a good idea for her to come to Austria.

I had changed. This trip had healed something in me that therapy, self-help books, or maybe even religion could never touch. I finally knew how to have fun and be with people who were very different from me. I also knew that the period in my life where I could have casual sex was over. Well, not over exactly, but almost. I knew that I wanted friendship, fun and fidelity from the next woman I fell in love with.

CHAPTER 7
GETTING A CLUE

"People talk about beautiful friendships between two persons of the same sex. What is best of that sort, as compared with the friendship of man and wife, where the best impulses and highest ideals of both are the same? There is no place for comparison between the two friendships; the one is earthly, the other divine."

Mark Twain, A Connecticut Yankee in King Arthur's Court

When I returned home I decided it was time to date again, but in a way I had never done before. I was ready to get off the crazy cycle of love—meeting, merging, separating, grieving, and moving on. I wanted to find someone I could be with as friends first, lovers second. I had never made love to a woman who was also my best friend. I had looked at women's bodies long enough, but now I wanted and needed to see something eternal. I yearned for a glimpse of the soul bare of makeup, the beauty that time only enhances. The only way to do this was to not jump in bed with every willing woman I went out with. All too often I slept with someone I had just met.

I read somewhere that if a person is attracted to ten people and dates all of them for three to six months without being sexually intimate, at the end of that period he or she would only be attracted to maybe three out of the ten. In other words, time and information dispels our fantasies if the blood stays in our brains instead of heading south. If we would only take our time, then we would make healthier choices about choosing a lifelong partner.

I knew this thinking was right. I couldn't count the number of times I had rushed into a sexual relationship with what I thought to be a wonderful woman. By the third month, I knew without a doubt that we were totally incompatible, except maybe sexually. Both of us would convince ourselves for a year or two that with time and several dozen hours of therapy we could make it work. That certainly was the case with Grace, my most recent tragic love affair. It took seven years before we threw in the tattered towel and called it quits. We had exhausted at least two therapists, not to mention dozens of friends, all who wished us well but knew long before we did there was no way in hell we would stay together. If asked, both of us would say we rushed into sex too soon.

When people become romantically involved, they hide huge parts of themselves. We tell only what the other wants to hear, and then six months later when they say something like, "I really don't know who you are," we wonder why. We tend to tell friends who we are, what we want, need, dream and hope for. In other words, we let them get to know the "real me." With would-be lovers, though, we tend to only show the good parts.

I started dating again (heavy sigh) at the tender age of 44. I promised myself I would do things differently. No matter how attracted I was to a woman, I was going to develop a friendship first, and search for the soul inside of the body.

First, there was Margaret Brown. She had hazel eyes, brown hair and was in her mid-thirties. She had never been married and was working on her master's degree in English literature. She had a similar sense of humor to mine, which is somewhat on the dark and deranged side, so we laughed a lot. We ate at expensive restaurants, went to the movies, and took long walks. We got to know each other gradually. In other words, we avoided sexual intimacy and courted.

By the twelfth date, I was glad we hadn't been intimate. I asked her the simple question, "Margaret, what do you really want out of a relationship?"

She looked at me as we sat across the table at Jeffrey's Restaurant, then looked away and said, "I don't have a clue."

I was stunned.

"Do you know what you want?" she said.

"I want someone to cherish and adore me, someone who wants to settle down and raise a family." We both knew she was not ready for that. We said goodnight at her door and I never saw her again. Years before I wouldn't have known what I wanted, so of course I would have been attracted to someone with a similar lack of direction. Now I was focused, and I didn't want to be with someone who wasn't.

I dated three or four other women and asked the same question, "What do you really want out of a relationship?" For the most part, I received the same answer, "I don't have a clue." Where were all the women who wanted an old-fashioned family? I began to think I had a defective picker. (I said "picker," not "pecker." Although I hadn't used it in a while, I was fairly sure it was still functioning properly.)

It was during this experimental phase that Susan and I began to deepen our friendship. She started writing after she returned from the island, and we began lengthy correspondences and one- and two-hour phone conversations. She was willing to go the distance to create a real friendship. I thought when we left the island that we might write once or twice and have a pleasant phone call now and then, but I was wrong. She made sincere efforts to deepen our friendship, and I was glad to reciprocate. Over the next eight months, she and I talked almost every night, and wrote at least one letter a week. She still dated her boyfriend and felt safe enough to talk to me about him and the difficulties they encountered as they tried to deepen their relationship. I kept her apprised of my efforts in the dating game. We talked as friends. We didn't hide or pretend to be other than what we were — two people who were trying to get it right.

Eventually she gave up on her beau, and I comforted her as best as I could. I was glad to support her during that difficult time. She knew she could count on me to be there for her as a friend, and I already included her on my list of true friends. Even though I was still attracted to her, I never held out hope for a romantic relationship. She'd made it clear in the beginning that she only wanted friendship, and I respected her wishes. Besides, the sixteen-year age difference between us prohibited any chance of a successful romance. I valued our friendship, and learned to ignore any thoughts of more.

Little did I know how much I was going to need her support. A temptation from my past was headed straight my way.

CHAPTER 8

A VISIT FROM AN OLD FRIEND

"Yesterday,
Life was such an easy game to play...
Oh, I believe in yesterday...
Why she had to go? I don't know..."
John Lennon and Paul McCartney

It was a beautiful autumn evening in Austin (temperature in the mid-80's), when from out of the blue I got a call from my high school sweetheart, Penelope Ann St. Claire. She said she was coming to Austin the next day for a visit and would like to get together and talk.

I needed a friend to talk to so I called Susan; I knew she would really listen. For over an hour I told Susan the long, painful story of my relationship with Penelope.

Penelope and I were students at the same high school, even though she lived in a town across the river from me. She was a cheerleader and president of her senior class. She was Miss Everything. I, on the other hand, was Mr. Nobody. I smoked and drank, hung out at pool halls, and tried to look as tough as possible so I wouldn't get the shit beat out of me. Penelope was a born-again Christian who sang solos in the church choir. I hadn't been to church since I was thirteen and heard a minister praise a mother for taking her restless infant out to the vestibule and spanking him. I got up, walked out, and kept on walking—I should say running—from God for years. I loved Penelope so much that I promised God if he let me have Penelope Ann St. Claire, then I would do anything he asked, even go back to church and become a minister like my mother always wanted.

God answered my prayer, or at least I thought he did. Penelope and I went together on and off for four years. Our relationship progressed from a deep, loving friendship to a romance so passionate it consumed both of us. She and I talked for hours about everything from life to death, from God to the Devil. Most importantly, I treated her differently than any other woman I'd been with. I respected her for her innate intelligence, her honesty, and her strong, abiding faith in a God who let me down more times than I cared to count. I respected, cherished, and adored her. I especially respected her for keeping her precious virginity when so many men, including myself, wanted to take it from her. Penelope took the time to see what lay beneath my crude exterior, the alcohol, the cigarettes, and the swagger, and loved the real me. Even her mom loved me. Penelope was the only woman, other than my mother, who prayed for my soul and my happiness.

Strangely, our relationship was characterized by breakups, all instituted by Penelope, who then dated more popular guys, such as the captain of the football team or the president of the senior class. These times were full of pain and confusion for me. I thought she loved me as much as I loved her, so why did she initiate these periodic breakups, especially right when our relationship was going so well? Perhaps it was because those guys didn't have bad reputations like I did. People claimed I screwed every girl that went out with me. I didn't, but I did nothing to discourage the rumors, except to Penelope. (Truth is, I didn't have my first sexual encounter until I was 18. I was trying to nail this majorette in the front seat of my 1971 yellow Dodge Dart Swinger and was so drunk that to this day I don't know if I made love to her or to my gear shift.)

Penelope and I ended up at the same college, where she was still a cheerleader and Miss Everything. I still drank, smoked grass, and went to church (yes, I made good on that promise). I even did a little lay preaching on the side when a minister got sick or traveled out of town. It's amazing what you can rationalize when you mix religion, booze, grass, and a hurting heart.

One night, in midst of another breakup, I was driving home from The Colony Men's Shop, a retail clothing store where I worked part time. Penelope had been dating another guy who owned a store in the new mall, and the thought of her with another man made me sick to my stomach. I made another promise to God: I would stop smoking and drinking if he'd just give me

Penelope for good. I was tired of the breakups. I wanted her to be mine forever. I wanted to marry her.

I rolled down the window of my Swinger, threw out the cigarettes, and never smoked again—cigarettes, I mean. I didn't manage to give up pot until quite a while later.

After throwing away the cigarettes, I was amazed when Penelope called that same evening and said she wanted to see me. She wanted to go out to dinner and talk. I agreed immediately, and when I picked her up that night, I could tell that something was different.

During dinner at our favorite restaurant, she said, "You know I've been dating Ross for several months. Well, we broke up and I was wondering if you and I could get back together. I'd like to stay together this time, for real."

I nearly choked on my food. I couldn't believe what she was saying. Was this a thousand prayers answered right here in this restaurant? I immediately said yes and for the next few weeks we were inseparable. We did everything together except make love. We had made out, but never gone all the way; for her it was not right or Christian.

After that night, I felt an increased desire to make love her, but I didn't push myself on her. She could tell I was ablaze with desire, and truth be known, she was, too. So one night after dinner, I took her to my mobile home and put on some soft music. No, it wasn't just music. It was Rod McKuen with the San Sabastian Strings, I remember it clearly. I was a romantic Alabama redneck whose floors were covered with red shag carpet and whose idea of classy furniture included imitation black leather.

I turned out the lights, except for the lava lamp, and we started kissing and heavy petting. We made out so long I got what was known as blue balls, which is redneck for wanting to screw so badly that your balls turn blue. (One night when I was 16, Penelope and I made out in the back seat of my 1961 burgundy Chevy convertible. I came home doubled over like someone had hit me hard in the stomach. My father recognized the symptoms and told me to go out and pick the back end of my car up and everything would be back to normal. I thought the guy was crazy, but I was hurting so bad I knew I had to try something. Much to my chagrin, it worked.)

But that night in my Alabama love shack on wheels with Rod McKuen in the background, I felt a pain that picking up the back of my car wouldn't cure. I wanted to make love to Penelope, and I wanted it to be forever.

I remember taking off everything but her panties and bra. Without any warning, she stood up and started to get dressed. She looked at me and said, "I never, ever want to see you again," and then she left.

For weeks I tried to call her but she wouldn't answer the phone. I couldn't believe she was serious. We'd broken up many times before, but that time was different. I was in mortal agony and terror.

I had not seen her again.

Susan listened to my story and never interrupted. Finally she asked me, "Why do you think Penelope didn't marry you?"

The only answer I could give was that she didn't love me.

"And you haven't talked to her since then?"

I explained that Penelope and I had talked a few times over the years, but I had always avoided the one thing I really wanted to know: Why did she leave?

Now it was time to get an answer to the question I had thought about more than God, family, and my future. At that moment, I felt as if I had no future until I got an answer and put it to rest.

I had to know why she left.

I thanked Susan for letting me bend her ear for so long. She was crying, saying it was one of the saddest stories she'd ever heard. I told her I would call the next night after my encounter with Penelope.

It may sound insane, but I loved Penelope Ann St. Claire like no other woman for twenty-five years. After she left me, I made sure I would never be vulnerable to a woman like her again. I consciously chose only women who were her opposites. She was a Christian; I dated pagans, Buddhists, atheists, agnostics, and other assorted sinners. She had blonde hair; I dated women with brown hair, red hair, gray hair, and hair as dark as night. Penelope was petite; I dated strong, outdoorsy, big-boned women. She was a Republican; I dated Democrats, communists, and socialists. She wanted children; I dated women who already had children and who didn't want more, or women who thought, as I did, that there were too many unwanted children in the world, so why bring in more? I stayed away from women who reminded me of her because I already thought of her a thousand times a day since I was sixteen years old.

Losing Penelope had been one of the most painful experiences of my life, and I had no wish to repeat it.

I pulled out the gold pocket watch that I wore every day. Penelope gave it to me for Christmas one year, the same year I gave her a stereo for her new apartment. Her initials were engraved on one side of the watch and my initials were on the other side. It was one of the most precious gifts I'd ever received. I had looked at it and rubbed it between my thumb and forefinger so often that the initials had faded. I stroked my fingers over it, and thought of the things we carry around with us. Twenty-five years is a long time.

Chapter 9

THE QUESTION AND THE ANSWER

"There are a thousand million questions."
The Moody Blues

Penelope called me when she got to town. "Hi John, I'm here. Austin is so beautiful, I can't believe it."

"I know, that's why I've lived here for fifteen years," I said, "but Lord, does it get hot here. You came at just the right time."

"So when can we get together?"

"How about tonight?" I said, so scared I was shaking.

"Tomorrow would be better for me."

"Okay, tomorrow it is. I'll pick you up and we'll go to dinner and talk. I'm really looking forward to seeing you."

"Me, too," she said.

"Give me directions," I said. "I'll see you at seven o'clock."

That night as I lay sleepless, I pictured Penelope as a young girl and clearly saw why I loved her so much: she had been my friend—my best friend. Penelope was the only woman I ever took the time to develop a friendship with first, before becoming more serious. It was no coincidence, then, that our breakup was the most painful of my life.

And in just a few more hours I would learn why she left me.

That evening I got dressed with all the self-consciousness of an adolescent going on his first date. Earlier in the day I had my car washed and cleaned. I wanted the evening to be perfect. I wanted her to see what she'd missed by leaving me; I wanted her to regret the years between us. I wanted her.

From the beginning, that night was different from any other we'd spent together. When I got to her friend's house she stood in the doorway waiting for me, something she never did when we were dating. I can't recall one single date when she didn't keep me waiting for a minimum of thirty minutes, and sometimes as long as an hour or more. By the time she was ready, I'd be so angry I could hardly talk.

But this time was different. This time she was ready, and there would be no waiting.

There she stood, so beautiful I couldn't take my eyes off her. She must have been older, heavier, but no matter how hard I looked, I only saw the young woman I remembered in my dreams. We offered each other a tentative embrace and left for dinner.

We had a wonderful meal overlooking the Colorado River in downtown Austin. Old cypress trees hung over the water as weeping willows danced in the breeze. I enjoyed being with her, talking to her. I couldn't ask the question yet; it had to wait until later.

Penelope told me about her three sons, now all in college. They were all straight-A students and the oldest was president of his senior class. The second was quarterback for his football team, and the third son was going to be a minister. She was very proud of them. I told her about my writing and teaching career. We laughed a lot, just like we used to.

Her tears began to flow when she started talking about her husband of twenty-five years who had recently died of leukemia. As it turns out, the tears were not so much about his death as by the lack of life they had shared. His greatest gift to her was her three boys; the greatest wound was his lack of love and passion for her. He was the only man she had ever "known," and now she didn't know what to do. She caught herself mid-emotion and dried her eyes with a napkin.

It was time to take her to my apartment and be alone with her. Time to ask the question.

After I gave her the short tour and introduced her to my cats, Lucy and Little Bit, I made us some coffee. We sat by the fireplace, though there was no fire. Even in October Texas is too hot for a fire. Penelope talked a little more about her boys and said a few things about her husband. Finally I popped the question, "Why did you leave me that night?"

She looked at me for a long time before saying anything. "Don't you know? How could you not know after all this time?"

"I've never known. I've thought about it thousands of times. We were so close."

"That's just it—we were too close."

"But you knew I wanted to marry you. It doesn't make sense. I loved you more than anyone or anything else in my life. Hell, I have never stopped loving you. Why didn't you love me?"

"Wait a minute. Do you think I didn't love you? John, I have always loved you. I love you right now." She calmly reached over, took my hand, and held it gently.

"What in the hell are you trying to do to me? You never loved me. You're making this up just to make me feel better. I'm half crazy with anger and hurt."

Penelope began to cry. "I left because I was terrified of the feelings I had for you. I was terrified of the passion you brought out in me, of what

I might have done that night. I was a good Christian girl scared of the feelings flowing through my body. So I left and closed the door on a kind of passion I wanted but was afraid of. Then I married a man who had almost no passion. But I can't say I made a mistake. How can I say that?" She pulled out her wallet from her purse and showed me the pictures of her handsome sons. "He gave me these." She looked at the pictures, then tucked them away. "But don't think I didn't love you."

"You didn't love me or you would have stayed with me." I started weeping. "For twenty-five years I've loved you, believing you didn't love me in return. Now all of a sudden I'm supposed to change my whole way of viewing us, my past, my world?"

In a calmer voice she said, "John, is it possible you convinced yourself I didn't love you in order to make our not being together more bearable? Then I would be guilty and you would be a victim of unrequited love, never having to open your heart again?"

"Fuck you, Penelope. Fuck you. If you're telling me the truth, I've lived my whole life believing a lie. I thought that if you couldn't love me, then no one else ever would. I gave everything to you, and you walked out. Now, after all these years, you're telling me you left with love in your heart, that you left because you were afraid?"

I stomped around the room, slung books at the wall, knocked over a lamp. "God damn you!"

"John, I know you must be upset, but please don't take the Lord's name in vain. I'm sorry I didn't tell you sooner, but I had no idea you were in such pain. I didn't realize you thought I didn't love you. You were so precious, so dear to me. You were my best friend. I can't tell you how many times I wanted to call you during these years. But I couldn't. I had the boys to think of. I took vows."

I calmed down a little bit and pulled out my pocket watch. "Do you remember giving me this?"

"Of course I do. I can't believe you still have it." She took the watch and rubbed her fingers over the initials, just as I had done countless times. She cried some more before handing it back to me. "John, I've always loved you. I'm sorry I hurt you. I'm sorry we didn't have a life together. And I'm very sorry that you never married. It's not too late, you know. You're still young. There are lots of women looking for a good man."

"How about you? Are you looking for a good man?"

"I don't know what I'm looking for. Arthur has been gone less than a year. I'm not even dating yet. Look at me, raising three sons has taken a toll. I'm not as pretty as the girl you remember."

I took a deep breath and held both of her hands. "Say you'll marry me right now. I'll put my stuff in the car and we'll go to my cottage in the Smoky Mountains. We'll love each other until the day we die. Say yes and we'll leave this evening."

Her face became hard, her voice serious. "John, I can't say yes. I don't know what I'm doing right now, much less with the rest of my life. I don't know if I'll ever marry again. My world is turned upside down. I have to think of the kids. Their father hasn't been in the ground more than seven months. I love you, but I don't know if you could ever forgive me."

"You always did think too much. You were scared then and you're scared now. Don't be. Just say yes."

She stood up. It was well past time to take her back to her friend's house. I held her sweater for her to put on. I closed my eyes and for just a moment, smelled her hair. It may have been gray, but it still smelled the same as in younger days.

We drove in complete silence out to the Hill Country, about twenty miles outside of Austin. I pulled into her friend's driveway just as it began to rain lightly. Penelope looked out the window and smiled a sad smile.

"I remember taking you home at night and sitting for hours in your driveway talking about everything under the moon," I said. For a while it seemed like no time or distance had ever been between us. I knew her in a way her husband never had, and despite the fact we were never lovers, she knew me more intimately than any other woman.

I kissed her ever so lightly, and then we held each other for a long time. She tried to look happy, but I felt the same sadness I always felt when we said goodnight. It was as if my life had come full circle. I didn't want another goodbye, not from her. Would we ever get together?

I watched in silence as she got out and walked to the house. I don't know what another man would have done. Maybe another man wouldn't let her go all those years ago; maybe another man wouldn't have let her go now. I didn't want to let her go; I wanted to lure her back to my Alabama love shack and pick up where we left off twenty-five years before.

I watched her, then got out of the car and said, "Just a minute, Penelope." I walked over to her and held her again. "I was insane when I asked you to come with me. Forgive me. And thank you for tonight."

She waved slowly and then she was gone. I knew that I would always love her.

CHAPTER 10
THE LIST

*"If I made a list of all the things that I wanted, I would
have settled for less than what I actually got."*
Alcoholics Anonymous

Weeks had passed since my meeting with
Penelope, and during that time I'd done a lot of
thinking. Although I still loved Penelope and
wanted to be with her, something changed inside
of me when I learned the truth about the past.

I have always had a love affair with The Past.
But Memory Lane is a cul-de-sac; it will only take
you so far, and the scenery never changes.

I've spent many waking hours examining
things that were said, not said, done, or left
undone. I often revisit schools, churches, hospitals,
and homes—all containers of my past. I walk the
hallways and inspect the rooms like a southern
Sherlock Holmes, looking for clues and keys that
may unlock the boxes in my mind—which usually
contain nothing but bad memories. But this time,
examining the past had paid off. There was a peace
in my heart where once there had been hurt and
anger. Penelope had not rejected me; she'd been
controlled by fear.

I needed to give Penelope one last call. I phoned her in November. As soon as I heard her voice, I could tell, "You still can't be with me, can you?"

"It's the kids. They just wouldn't understand me rushing into another man's arms so soon after their father's passing. I know you can't wait on me, but maybe if some more time went by then we could start seeing each other occasionally. Would that work for you?"

"Pen, I've waited long enough. I need someone who isn't afraid to love me. I wish that could be you, but it's not. You will always be my first love, but now I need more than a ghostly lover. I hope you find a lover and friend that will bring out all the passion that's remained unused inside of you. You're still so beautiful. You're going to make some man count his blessings."

Her voice cracked with emotion. "I'm sorry I couldn't say yes twenty-five years ago, and I'm sorry I can't say yes now. You're always in my prayers, and I'll always love you."

"I'll always love you, too," I said, and gently hung up the phone.

Once again I called Susan, this time telling her how I'd let Penelope go. Her support helped me through that difficult time, and I was thankful for her friendship.

After several more weeks, I had a life-changing conversation with my friend Bill Stott (remember the guy who goaded me into going on vacation?) Well, he came up with another bright idea. "John, why don't you put an ad in the Austin Chronicle. I put one in several months ago and met tons of women."

"Did you like any of them?"

"No, but I had some fun, and it helped me learn what I don't want in a woman. Have you ever just sat down and made a list of the qualities you want in a woman, what you like and don't like, what you can't live without? You ought to try it sometime."

"Well, no, I haven't done that. I've suggested that others do it, but I never did. Maybe I will, but as far as running an ad, I don't think I'm ready for that."

"I remember a man who wasn't ready to go to Club Med, either."

"Kiss my ass. I hate it when you're right. I'll make the damn list and put it in the Chronicle. Happy?"

"Delighted. Someday you'll thank me, old man."

I got out a pen and paper, and what I wrote both shocked and scared me:

1. She must go slow to see if we can be friends first

2. A woman who is smart

3. Beautiful

4. Wants to have a family

5. Has a deep sense of her own spirituality

6. A woman who is introspective — willing to look at her own flaws and to get help when necessary.

7. Independent

8. Has a good sense of humor

9. Adventurous

10. Has her own source of income (professional, but open to quitting her job once we had children if it became necessary)

At the bottom of the list, I wrote in big letters:
S U S A N

I called Bill. "Guess what? I made the list. Now I'm sadder than before. I can't believe it, but Susan is this list — exactly. I can't tell you how many times I've stared at her picture, and every time I do, I feel guilty and dishonest. So I threw her picture in the garbage can. I'm going to stop drooling over it and just be her friend." I felt stupid and old, very old.

Bill's voice was gentle. "Well, at least now you know what you want. If it can't be Susan, then you can look for those same qualities in the women you meet from now on. Maybe you should go ahead and place your ad — and make sure you keep that list."

He was right. I was glad I made the list. "I'll call the paper tomorrow," I said.

It felt strange to acknowledge the depth of my feelings for Susan. I didn't want to be dishonest with her, but I was afraid if she discovered how much I desired her, she would end our friendship, and that was a precious relationship to me. Besides, a romantic relationship really wasn't feasible. With our age difference, we wouldn't have much in common. So she liked the beach? Everybody likes the beach. She wanted to paint? I wanted to write. Two artistic personalities make a chaotic household. It obviously wouldn't work.

I found the phonebook and jotted down the newspaper's number at the top of my list. First thing in the morning I'd make the call, and get serious about finding Mrs. Right because, after all, the holidays were quickly approaching.

CHAPTER 11
HOLIDAY PLANS

*"Man is such a reasonable being that he can find
a reason to do whatever he likes."*
Benjamin Franklin

Let's see…a sharp pointed stick in the eye or going home for the holidays? Difficult choice.

For years, during the holiday season I felt like Sisyphus. He was the mythological king who rolled a huge boulder up the mountain, only to have it roll back down and have to start all over. Only I had three boulders: Thanksgiving, Christmas, and New Year's. The depression that dogged me through the holiday season made my life a living hell.

To offset the accompanying depression, I usually visited friends or went to the movies — and I mean every day. Years earlier I'd learned that spending the holidays with my parents only compounded the depression. Every time I went home I went into what psychologists call regression. In other words, while I made the plans to go home, I was in my forties. By the time I got on the plane, I was emotionally in my twenties; and by the time my mother met me at the airport, I was headed back to my teens. By the time I reached my parent's house and had one short conversation with my father, I'd be looking for a womb to crawl back into.

Now I know this phenomenon doesn't happen to everyone. There are sub-species of the human race who are psychologically mature enough to return home and remain their true chronological age. I don't actually know many people like this, but legend has it they exist — somewhere.

One day an old college sweetheart, Trisha, called me on a whim to see what I had been doing for twenty years. She invited me to spend Thanksgiving with her, and so I, thinking I might have an avenue of escape from holiday depression, happily accepted her offer.

I felt a little guilty accepting Trisha's offer, especially since I'd just realized the depth of my feelings for Susan, not to mention the emotional roller coaster of seeing Penelope again. But neither of those relationships were remote possibilities, and I wanted to move on with my life. Besides, Trisha and I had a lot in common. We were the same age and came from the same part of the country, and I was curious about the possibility of us hitting it off again. I was crazy about her when we were in college. Trisha wasn't the love of my life, but she was a damn good stand-in, especially while I waited for Penelope to stop dating other guys and get back around to me. Trisha had been beautiful, and, like Penelope, I'd always wanted to make love to her but never had gotten a chance. Now she was divorced, had no children, and was living in Birmingham, Alabama.

A few days later I flew to Birmingham. Trisha had hardly changed. She was small, beautiful, and looked ten years younger than her age. In short, she was gorgeous. As soon as I came down the jet-way, she ran and threw her arms around me. She looked at me as if only a day had passed since we last saw each other.

"Trisha, you haven't changed a bit. You look great."

"You're not looking close enough, but thank you for the compliment. How was your flight?"

"Great. God, it is good to see you. It's been a long time." I looked at her and thought, this could be the one. It would be so nice to share a common history and background. Still, a part of me was aware that this 43-year-old woman would not be having any children, which meant she wouldn't fulfill an important goal on my list. I quickly told that voice to shut the hell up.

We talked about the past as we drove to her lovely home in Brookhaven Heights. When we arrived at her house, she showed me around. It was decorated like a Martha Stewart magazine — comfortable, fashionable, and inviting. Her big four-poster bed looked especially inviting, I thought, as I felt myself slipping on an old familiar slope.

"This will be our bed while you're here. I don't mean to seem pushy, but from the moment you got off that plane, I knew I wanted to make love to you. Can you handle all of this forwardness?"

"Uh, yeah."

What happened to all the friends first and being cherished and adored stuff? I must have packed them in a bag the airlines lost. It had been nearly a year since I had been with a woman, and I didn't have the will, or lack of good manners, to insult my hostess by asking for another room.

Looking back, I think depression was a large factor in my poor decision. The holidays were always a difficult time for me, and after everything I'd been through in the last year, I needed to feel loved and desired, even if only for a weekend. I consoled my conscience by saying Trisha and I had been friends years before, so I wasn't really breaking my promise to myself.

Trisha and I had a great time. We spent two days making love; Trisha was a passionate, generous lover. The rest of the time we ate, watched movies, took long walks, and reminisced about old friends. On Thanksgiving Day she fixed me breakfast in bed, and we went to a movie. She made a lovely dinner that evening, and afterwards we made love.

But my lovemaking was like most of my lovemaking in the past, more performance than presence, and more technique than tenderness.

Somehow, I wasn't there. She seemed satisfied, but from the moment we first made love, I knew she was not The One.

With Trisha, I began realizing that having sex was what I'd always done, and what I'd always settled for. I knew how to fuck, how to perform the role of a good sex partner. What I had never learned was how to give and receive love—how to make love. Sex was no longer good enough. I wanted love. And I didn't love Trisha.

"John, I haven't been with a man since me and my husband divorced over two years ago. He was the only man I'd ever been with. I didn't know that lovemaking could be so much fun. This was great, don't you think?"

"Absolutely. I'm glad you called and invited me for the holidays."

On the last day, as I was packing and getting ready to leave, Trisha began crying. "I'm going to miss you, Sweetie. I was wondering if we could spend Christmas together, if you don't already have plans." Her soft hands pulled on mine as we said goodbye.

I took a deep breath and said yes before I even knew I had done so. Why did I say yes? Why didn't I tell her the truth? I have no idea, especially since saying yes undermined everything I was working towards. And for some unknown reason, I kept up the pretense of wanting a relationship with her, even though I knew I was hurting both of us. "How about I fly into Birmingham on Christmas Eve?" I said. "We can drive up to my cabin in Mentone and spend the weekend there. I have a huge fireplace and we can just stay inside and tell jokes, read, and who knows, maybe even make love once or twice. What do you say?"

She blushed. "I'd rather you come here again, if you don't mind."

"Sounds like a good plan."

She drove me to the airport. I got my bags out of her trunk and we kissed for a long time. I kept thinking, here I go again, back to old behavior patterns. I knew I didn't love this woman. I liked her, but I didn't love her. I failed to put building a strong friendship before fulfilling sexual needs. I was breaking my promise to myself.

At a friend's party a few years ago, I met a man named Rod Wilkins. He was in his eighties and said that if a man my age was still "sport fucking," then he was still trying to prove something to somebody. I overheard Rod having a conversation with a guy in his mid- to late thirties. "If you aren't certain that you and the woman you're with are committed to each other, then you have no business having sex. You're old enough to know that lovemaking is what a mature man does. A mature man courts a woman, and doesn't become intimate unless he's willing to make a commitment."

I don't know the man's name that Rod was talking to, but he kept saying, "I just don't agree, Rod. There's nothing wrong with fucking as many women as possible if every one of them is agreeable."

That guy didn't hear Rod. I did. Rod was old enough to remember how to court a woman. I had not been able to put his knowledge into practice yet, but at least I knew he was right.

Rod's wise words floated back to me now, and I was sad that I hadn't applied his wisdom to my own life. I went back to Austin. Trisha and I called each other every night. After I hung up, I called Susan. The conversations with Trisha kept getting shorter and shorter, and the intimate talks with Susan kept getting longer and longer.

About ten days before Christmas, Susan asked if I had plans for the holiday. I kept skirting the issue for as long as I could. I finally told her I was going to be with Trisha for Christmas.

Susan got real quiet for a few moments, then said, "Do you think there's still something between you two?"

I had told her about my past relationship with Trisha and spending Thanksgiving with her. "I honestly don't know," I said, lying more to myself than to her. Maybe Trisha and I had a chance, and maybe I wasn't making a huge mistake.

"Have you made plans for New Year's Eve yet?" she asked.

"No."

"Why don't you come to Miami and spend New Year's with me and my family?" she asked.

"Hon, while I consider you one of my dearest friends and it is so wonderful of you to invite me, I just wouldn't feel comfortable since I haven't met your parents. I wouldn't want them to get the wrong impression about us."

"First of all, let me worry about their impression. Second, I don't want you spending the holiday all by yourself. And third, I'd really like to see you."

"I'd like to see you, too. But why don't you come to Austin instead?"

"Settled," she said. "Austin, New Year's Eve, great!"

We said goodbye, and a week later I flew to Birmingham.

CHAPTER 12
THE FROSTED WINDOW PANE

"Have a holly, jolly Christmas."
Burl Ives

As soon as I saw Trisha standing at the gate, something, I can't say what exactly, went out of me. To make matters worse, she saw that same something fly out of me, and there was nothing I could do to fake it. We kissed for just a brief moment, the kind you give a sister, or a mother, or an ex-girlfriend.

As we rode to her house, we chatted away like we didn't remember that moment at the gate. Trisha made light conversation, things like, "How was your trip?" and "Was it cold in Austin when you left?" When she pulled into her driveway, I noticed she'd decorated her house with candles in the windows and a large wreath on the door.

I tried to pretend I was happy to be there, but finally, she said, "John, is there something wrong? You don't seem the same. Has something happened?"

I avoided her eyes and said, "No, there's nothing wrong. It's just that Christmas is a hard time for me. I never really liked it much as a kid. My dad was always drunk and my mother was always making up excuses and stories for him. Christmas has always seemed sad, that's all."

"Let's see if we can't change that this year. Help me turn on the lights and put the angel on top of the tree. I've been waiting for you to do that."

Everything about her was perfect. I could have asked her for anything and she would have given it to me. I felt cherished and adored. After we lit the tree and I put the angel on top, I slowly undressed her. Her clothes floated off like fall leaves on a windy day. I picked her up and carried her to her four-poster bed and tried to make love to her as if I meant it, but couldn't.

Afterwards, I lay there and stared at the frosted windowpane. Every so often a drop of water rolled down the window's cold, flat face. The slow, fluid motion mesmerized me.

I couldn't look at Trisha for a long time. When I finally did, tears were running down her face. I wiped them away with my fingers and brushed her hair out of her eyes. "I'm sorry," I said.

"There's nothing to be sorry about. I loved our lovemaking. You were just a little distracted. People can't experience mountain tops every time they make love." She announced that she was going to take a shower and fix dinner. "Then we'll go to bed and tomorrow will be Christmas. It'll be great."

The moment from the airport was back, and she tried hard to deny it, but I couldn't. I shouldn't be there, but I didn't know how to say it. So I pretended for a while, then did the only thing I knew to do.

I don't even remember what the fight was about. She said something, and I pounced on it like a cat with a bag full of catnip. I jumped on every word she said. That night we slept in separate beds. In the middle of the night, she came in, woke me up, and told me to get out of her house; she never wanted to see me again. I got up, called a cab, and went to the nearest hotel. I couldn't sleep, so I wrote a poem about the last night that Trisha and I spent together.

NOISY SILENCE
There is a kind of noisy silence
some marriages make. Husbands
become devoted to it, and it makes
vows squeak like a rusty
front porch swing. A woman
lies next to a quiet man
for twenty or thirty years
alone in the dark. His breathing
turns her body into stone. She
seldom sleeps. She stares
at the ceiling and remembers how
she married young, and "for love."
Now she just waits for morning.

Sometime later, I wrote Trisha a letter and apologized for the fight. I let her know that it had nothing to do with her, and everything to do with me. She wrote me back, kindly wishing me well and thanking me for the short time we had spent together. She didn't want to be judgmental, she said, but she thought I was a little nuts because, "I would have taken such good care of you."

CHAPTER 13
THE CONVERSATION

"I'm not following you, I'm looking for you.
There's a big difference."
Martin Stett to Caul, The Conversation

After the Christmas fiasco with Trisha, I called Susan and told her everything that happened.

"Well, I wish I could say that I'm sorry, but I can't," she said.

I sat in stunned silence. It was the first time she hadn't fully supported me. I didn't know what to say.

She took a deep breath. "There is something I've wanted to ask you for some time, but I just haven't gotten the courage to do it. I think I know the answer already, but if I don't ask... I just need to know."

I was suddenly scared. What could she want to ask me? "What is it?"

"You remember the poem by the Persian poet, Rumi? One line really struck me: 'The breeze at dawn has secrets to tell you/Don't go back to sleep./You must ask for what you really want/Don't go back to sleep'." As she recited one of my favorite poems, I noticed how different her timing and inflection were compared to mine. It was almost as if she was reciting the words to her favorite song. "We've become friends, very good friends, right?" she said.

"Yeah, I feel like I can tell you anything. So what did you want to ask?" The suspense was agonizing. I wondered if I really wanted to hear her question.

"John," she said rather firmly, as if she were bracing herself, "if I don't ask you this, I...I don't want to go back to sleep. I have to ask for what I really want." Her voice trembled, and she hesitated for a minute. "Are you interested in me in a way other than as a friend? Because I would like to pursue a romantic relationship with you and see where it would go." She said the last part quickly, the way you rip off a Band-Aid.

My mouth dropped to my feet; my head spun like a top. "You are saying that you're interested in me romantically?" My words were slow and deliberate. I wanted to make sure I wasn't dreaming.

"Yes," she whispered.

I didn't say anything. I couldn't say anything.

Several moments passed. Susan started to speak again. Her voice was much lower and less confident. "If you aren't interested, I'll understand. I hope we can still be close friends."

"I thought you only wanted to be friends."

I think she sensed the disbelief in my voice and knew I wasn't searching for a polite way to reject her. "We are friends. I know you in a way I've never known another man. Now I want more."

I couldn't speak. I never expected this.

"John, are you still there?"

"Yes," I said, sounding more like a question than an answer. I took a deep breath and exhaled all of my anticipation, "The answer is definitely yes."

I heard Susan's sigh of relief, then a little giggle. "Really?" she asked.

"Yeah," I laughed nervously. "In fact, my friend Bill suggested I write down a list of everything I wanted in a woman. You were everything on the list. It made me sad because I thought you only wanted to be friends, and I didn't want to find someone else."

"I can't believe it!" she squealed. "I made a list, too. That's what made me decide to ask you. You are my list. At first, I felt the same way you did. I thought, why John? We're just friends. He doesn't think of me that way. But then I asked myself, Why not John? What could it hurt to ask?"

I couldn't believe my ears. "So let me get this straight, you're saying you want to pursue a romantic relationship with me—right?"

"That's right," she said with a new resolve.

"When did you first suspect this?"

"Honestly? Do you remember the first day we met at Club Med? I told you I was in a relationship, and I was just there to have a good time?"

"Of course I remember. You said you weren't there to have a romantic tryst, and you were going to be faithful to your boyfriend back home."

"That's exactly what I said. I must have met at least a dozen men on the island, and I told every one of them the same thing, but they all kept hitting on me anyway. You were the only one who heard what I said and respected me enough to honor it. I was awed that you honored me enough to accept that all I could offer you was friendship."

She started giggling.

"What?" I asked.

She giggled even more.

"What?" I asked more loudly.

"It's just that the one man content to be my friend, was the one man I wanted more from."

The way she said it was so deliciously mischievous I could hardly stand it.

She cleared her throat. "It was like you wanted to know me beyond my looks or the possibility of having sex. That is something I've never experienced before. You and I started a friendship based on respect and I found that very attractive."

Don't ask me how, but I knew she was smiling. Susan recognized she had the upper hand and was relishing my uneasiness. "So, do you think of me as a romantic possibility?" she asked.

"I do," I said. "From the moment I first laid eyes on you, I knew you were special, and I wanted to know you. I'm just so taken aback that you're attracted to me — I don't even have words."

"I'm sick of playing games. You've been an incredible friend. You've been as open and honest with me as any man has ever been. Since we already know each other, there's no need to pretend to be things we're not.

"Before we go any further," she continued, "I have to ask you a couple of questions. First, do you want a girlfriend, or a lifelong partner that will stick with you through thick and thin?"

"A partner," I said. I couldn't believe how direct and bold she was. It was wonderful.

"I shouldn't ask these questions so soon, but I need to know, are you open to the possibility of marriage?"

"Absolutely," I said, emphasizing each syllable.

"Okay," she said, "now for the really tough question."

"I'm ready," I said, hoping it was true.

"Do you want to have children?"

"Very much."

"Great!"

We were both feeling more at ease, but there was still so much more to say.

"Let me catch my breath," I said. "In the course of one phone conversation we've gone from being friends to talking about romance, marriage, and babies."

"I know, John," she said softly. "I don't want to rush into anything, but I wanted you to know how I feel about you."

"I need to ask you a question, too. Isn't our age difference going to be a problem?"

"No," she answered calmly. "It's not uncommon for Latin women to be with older men. It's even considered preferable. Older men are more experienced, and they know how to treat a woman."

"Until now, I've only thought of my age as a liability in the dating world; I never thought of it as a benefit," I said.

It's true that men slow down with age, but at least then they might be more willing to take the time to court a woman. Many younger men are too hot and impatient. The age difference between Susan and myself could actually be a benefit!

"Remember when we danced to Sade's 'Smooth Operator' and Sting's 'Fields of Gold' in the Caribbean?" she asked.

"Of course."

"When we danced, you held me like you'd never let me go, like I was yours. It wasn't inappropriate because that was your style of dancing." She took a deep breath. "Your embrace was strong, reliable, and respectful. Your touch told me you were tired of playing games and telling lies, and you wouldn't cling out of neediness. You looked into my eyes like you really wanted to see me, not just yourself reflected back."

"How did you get so damn wise?"

She laughed. "Guess it's the good company I keep."

"Yeah well, I've never dated a woman this much younger than me."

Susan thought for a minute, then asked, "How did those relationships work out?"

"Not great," I admitted.

"Then maybe it's time for a change."

"Maybe so."

"John, I feel really good about our conversation tonight."

"Me, too. I'm really looking forward to spending New Year's Eve with you."

"I can't wait. I have a very good feeling about us, but worse case, we go back to just being friends. Okay?"

"Okay, but I still can't believe it."

"Just one more thing—respect from a man means more to me than anything, and I've felt it from the first moment I met you. Your respect for me is one of the greatest gifts I've ever received. What gift do you need more than anything else?"

"I need someone who will cherish and adore me, someone who loves both herself and me enough to go very slowly. I hope you don't laugh at this, but I want to do something that's gone out of style. I want to really court you, and not hurry into a sexual relationship."

Without a pause she said confidently, "I can do that."

All I could say was, "Wow."

The words "I can do that" were wrapped with tenderness and tied with a ribbon that has been seen only a few times in this world. We had talked and opened our hearts to each other, yet several questions remained. Would I be able to court her, woo her? The magnitude of what I wanted to do— to love her and build a life together based on friendship—meant the possibility of failure loomed before me. It was as if I stood before a great chasm, and with one leap I would either gain the whole world or lose it. I felt both exhilarated and terrified.

Another question would prove more critical, though I didn't know it at the time. Would I *allow* a woman to cherish and adore me? Could I receive the gift that I've longed for, and grieved over not having?

CHAPTER 14

"Should old acquaintance be forgot..."

Susan and I had talked and written to each other for over six months. Before she asked The Question, our conversations had been platonic, practical, philosophical, spiritual, sublime, even ridiculous, but always respectful. After that conversation, the tone changed. There was a bit of sexual innuendo and a double entendre here and there. Our conversations weren't racy enough to be classified as phone sex, but I could feel both the phone and certain parts of my body heating up when we talked. Just the possibility of being sexually intimate with Susan was enough to accomplish that, but the feelings were compounded because I felt I knew the "real" Susan so well from our letters and conversations. As New Year's Eve and our first real date approached, the dialogue turned towards the possible. Yet I knew I had to court her before I allowed the sparks to turn into flame, so I didn't allow myself to dwell on sexual fantasies of us together. I was committed to beginning this relationship with reverence and reserve.

Finally New Year's Eve came, and I went to the airport to pick her up. It was the start of a three-day weekend I will never forget. She came down the jet way and floated into my arms. Her effervescent charm swept over me like a warm Texas wind in wintertime. She was so beautiful, and her smile must have broken the heart of every other man in the building. She was shorter than I remembered, but she had the radiance and energy of a nuclear reactor. I presented her with a dozen roses, and we walked out to the parking lot hand in hand. When we got to my car, I dropped her bags, and she kissed me in a way that let me know how much she had been anticipating this moment.

At my apartment she acted with a forthrightness I hesitate to describe. In my living room, she laughed, complimented me on this couch, that table, the African wall mask, and started removing her clothes—and I mean all of them. My eyes widened with shock. I sank down on the complimented couch. As she removed her underwear, I drank in every liquid moment, every inch of her quivering body. Saying nothing, I picked her up and carried her to my bed. She lay down on the black comforter and parted her legs like the Red Sea, then began rolling all over the bed as if saying, *This is my bed now, my room, and my man, regardless of who has been here before.* It was not a seduction, but a symbolic representation of her intentions. She was taking possession and marking her territory.

Suffice it to say, she was not going to leave Austin or me with anything less than a clear picture of her intentions, and, my God, what a picture. I've been around the block more times than a

Jehovah's Witness, and I've never seen anything like that before. Susan was a conservative Christian who had been saving herself for the right man, and to witness her display of raw sensuality shocked even me.

To this day, I don't have the faintest idea how I avoided ravishing her while she lay nude on my bed. Although Susan and I hugged and kissed, caressed, talked quietly, and laughed all night, we did not consummate our relationship—six more months would pass before that happened.

But even now, when I think of her, she's forever laying naked and squirming on that bed.

That weekend I showed her Austin. We ate in my favorite restaurants, walked the three and a half mile heart of the Hike and Bike Trail, danced at the Soap Creek Saloon, and delved ever more deeply into each other's hearts and souls. We laughed, cried, shared our strengths, and bared our weaknesses to each other.

Her Ecuadorian heritage was evident in her love of sexy Latin music, her choice of foods, and her spontaneity. She identified much more with her mother's Latin roots than her father's Indiana, Midwest ways. I loved this about her and found her Latina passions balanced my redneck, southern Appalachian slowness. We were good together.

We decided she would come back to Austin in April and stay with me to see if she liked me and the city enough to move from her beloved Miami.

After she went home, I called my friend Bill and told him about Susan's visit. He was ecstatic. "See, big boy, you never know what's going to happen. I'm delighted. What are you going to do now?"

There was a long pause. "I don't know. I never expected any of this. I think I'm still in shock."

"Well, I'm not. You've done nothing but talk about Susan since you returned from the island. I think you're damn lucky," he said.

I thought so, too.

CHAPTER 15

APRIL FOOL'S

"Are we just April Fools who can't
see all the danger around us?
When you smiled I looked into your eyes,
and I knew I'd be loving you."
Burt Bacharach and Hal David, April Fools

Susan was due to arrive in Austin on April first. I stood in the airport, palms sweaty, mouth dry, my heart beating like Secretariat's at the Kentucky Derby. As I waited for a glimpse of her, I thought April Fool's was a poor choice to plan her arrival. It would be the cruelest of all hoaxes if she didn't show up. After all, she'd had more than three months to rethink her decision to move in with me. Maybe she'd found someone new, someone younger. Maybe a friend had advised her to back out of the relationship. Maybe she didn't want to saddle herself with an old redneck like me. I waited for the call that said it was just a joke, Happy April Fool's.

I was scared about other things, too. I didn't have a clue as to how I was going to cohabitate with her. It had been a long time since I had, as Jeremiah Johnson (played by Robert Redford) said, "a full-time overnight woman."

Finally she arrived. She ran into my arms and we shared a big kiss. I handed her a dozen yellow roses, the official Welcome-To-Texas flower, and we headed to my apartment. I should have felt relieved, but for some reason, the feeling of fear in my stomach didn't quiet down. Truth was, we were both scared, but my fear ran deeper and stronger. Susan had not written books like *The Flying Boy*, *The Flying Book II: The Journey Continues*, and *The Flying Boy Book III*, each about my fears of commitment and opening up my heart to another person. Before I met Susan, I had promised myself there would be no more Flying Boy books. It was time to make good on that promise.

In my apartment the first thing Susan and I had to do was negotiate space, particularly closet space. She required a lot of it. I couldn't believe all the clothes she had, and I was a little shocked at the style, too. Miami clothes.

For the uninitiated, Miami is another country. The fact that it is in the United States is just a technicality. It's a hot, sweaty melting pot where Latinos rule, salsa music plays all night, and people go to work in tank tops, shorts, and sandals year round. Disco isn't in, you say? Miami didn't get the memo.

To be a fashionable Latina in Miami, your clothes must be stylish, form fitting and/or transparent, and worn with little or no undergarments. Which is fine, until you leave the loud, chaotic womb of South Florida and decide to go somewhere else, like, say, Austin, Texas.

I remember walking with Susan one day into Whole Foods Grocery. I looked at the people walking around us: long skirts, no makeup, lots of sensible shoes like Birkenstocks and Timberland. They dressed completely opposite of South Beach Miami, where clothing is made up of just enough material to make a handkerchief and where women wear high heels, makeup, and jewelry to bed. Always. No joke. It's the law.

To Susan, the people at granola central were probably just health nuts and thus were totally out of step with fashion. But then we went to other places—dinner, the movies, downtown. I think she began to notice a pattern. Everyone wore the wrong clothes. Austin was just one large fashion faux pas. She saw plain, vanilla people in dire need of emergency makeovers.

The whole fashion issue came to a head a few days later.

Susan told me that she wanted to continue the psychotherapy she had started in Miami. I suggested she might want to see my psychotherapist. She assured me that this wasn't going to work since he was a man, he wasn't Latin, and he was from Austin. "He won't get me," she said. I began to think she might be right, but she decided to give him a try anyway. I gave her the directions as she got dressed. I became a little codependent as she approached the door. I stopped her before she could turn the knob.

"Whoa!"

"What?" she turned, looking puzzled.

"You're not going to wear that, are you?"

She looked down at her black spandex micro mini skirt with matching bolero jacket, high-heeled sandals, and bare legs. "Yes, why? I shaved my legs."

My eyes widened.

She went to the mirror and checked herself out. "Everything matches. What's wrong?"

"I know it's none of my business, but you're barely dressed!"

"Oh, come on," she snorted.

I took a deep breath, knowing I was in danger-ous territory. "This," I said as I waved a hand up and down in front of her, "is inappropriate."

"Inappropriate? But I'm wearing black." In Miami, anything black is considered conservative.

We bantered back and forth until I came to my senses and offered my sincere apologies for getting into her business. I opened the door for her, and she left to see Dr. Maynard.

When she returned from her session, she said, "When I was sitting in the doctor's waiting room,

I thought to myself how silly you are. I've been dressing like this since I was a teenager. Everyone I know dresses like this. What's the big deal? Then my peripheral vision caught some movement to my left. A little girl, who looked about seven, was staring at me. I smiled back. Obviously, she appreciated haute couture. But before I could go into full gloat, her mother stepped in and took her by the arm. She gave me a quick once over and said very apologetically, 'I'm sorry. I've told her not to stare.' Stare? Wait a minute, what was going on here? Before I could think about it, the receptionist told me the doctor was ready to see me. Still a little shaken—and nervous about meeting your psychiatrist—I walked in. He wasn't what I expected. He was younger than I imagined and made me feel comfortable right away. We were about fifteen minutes into the session when it suddenly dawned on me: I was wearing a spandex micro mini skirt in a psychiatrist's office. I realized Dorothy wasn't in Kansas, I wasn't in Miami, and my one-dimensional wardrobe would have to include both cloth and color. My face started to burn with embarrassment. If Doctor Maynard noticed it, he hid it well. I tried several times, unsuccessfully, to pull down my skirt as much as possible. When that didn't work, I said something about how hot it was and took off my bolero jacket and draped it over my legs. Which was great from the waist down, but then I realized I was wearing an ultra skintight tee-shirt that wasn't exactly opaque." She paused and sighed. "I'm going to be run out of Austin."

"Sweetie, Austin is very different from Miami. We're into clothes, lots of them. But I want you to know that it's none of my business what you wear. I'm sorry for interfering. Please forgive me. It won't happen again."

A few days later, she asked me where she could go shopping to get some Austin clothes. I gladly took her to one of Austin's most popular dress shops, Chico's. She seemed to like the patterns and textures of the clothes, but there was so much material in them. (There is no Chico's in Miami.) You could tell by the look on her face that she wasn't crazy about wearing a skirt that actually went below her knees, but after her experience with Doctor Maynard, she thought she should try to fit in. Just a little.

Besides clothes shopping, Susan and I spent our first month in Austin learning to communicate. For example, I discovered that when she said, "I'm going to Target to get some things for the kitchen," meant she was going to be gone for three hours and come back with four hundred dollars worth of kitchen gadgets. She couldn't believe I was over forty years old and had written more books about failed relationships, three, than I had pots to cook in, two.

Also, Susan had to get used to my traveling. She knew I traveled a lot, but knowing about it and living with it were two different things. The entire experiment was especially difficult for Susan, since up until then she had lived with her parents. A great number of Latin women stay in the home until they are married, no matter how old they are. This was very difficult for me to understand, since I moved out when I was seventeen. I would have left by age seven if I could have gotten a job, a car, and an apartment with a lock on the front door that my parents couldn't bypass.

Susan was used to having lots of family around. People in Latin families not only tolerate each other, but also enjoy being in each other's company, for the most part. This was the opposite of my family and those of most of the women I had dated. To say that solitude was not Susan's best friend would be an understatement. She was both afraid and saddened to be left alone. She had been brave to move so far from all that she knew, but being left alone was pushing her limits. She was angry, confused and frustrated. So whenever I had to be out of town, I learned to write daily emails, leave notes for her to find around the house, send flowers, and phone often.

Austin was a great turning point in our relationship because it took us out of the chaos of distance dating into the beautiful new reality of being together. It was a time for negotiation, compromise, patience, and love. I think we both knew within two weeks of our Austin experiment that we loved each other—truly and maturely. She listened to me; she was sweet and attentive, and told me I was smart and funny. How could I help falling in love with her? And me? Well, I could only assume she found some redeeming features in this old Alabama boy.

CHAPTER 16

DIAMONDS AND TRUCKS

"Diamonds are a girl's best friend."
Leo Robin

Susan and I spent the next several months drawing closer and closer. One evening we were cuddling on the couch after dinner and sharing "what ifs" about marriage and kids. I said, "I want you to know I don't believe in spending money on a diamond ring."

Susan's look suggested I had just admitted to being a serial killer.

"What, no diamond? You've got to be kidding. See this finger?" She wiggled her ring finger. "This finger was made for a diamond, mister. What the hell are you thinking?"

"It's too expensive and materialistic. It doesn't fit my principles."

"Well, it fits mine."

She pulled away from me and I could see I had sunk in her estimation. But I couldn't help it; I was a recovering hippie.

I'm a product of the cultural revolution of the Sixties, when jeans and a tee-shirt were considered formal attire, and, while love wasn't exactly free, it was relatively inexpensive. (And yes, I inhaled as often as I could.) The Sixties were clear about things like diamond rings and ostentation and chastity and permanent waves and permanent anything: they were to be avoided at all costs. How was I to give up beliefs I had not only learned, but espoused?

Later that summer, Susan and I went to a horrible movie. It was so dismal and such a waste of time that it must have set an impatient burr in my flesh, because on the ride home I found myself blurting out, "Look, I'm not in any hurry to get married. I want to take it slow. Maybe we should get married in six months or in a year or two."

Susan glared out the passenger window with a look that said, What kind of ride is this man taking me on?

After several minutes she spoke. She seemed to choose her words carefully. "I can understand waiting six months or a year. I'm fine with that. We've known each other now for nearly a year. But if all this takes longer than a year I will be very concerned."

I glanced over at her and met her blue-green eyes. She wasn't going to push me or belittle me for taking my time, but I could tell she was worried about my ability to make a commitment.

Susan was beginning to discover that she was in love with a Contrary. You tell me I have to walk; I'll drive. Tell me to sleep; I'll stay awake. But this time when I looked into Susan's eyes, I didn't feel Contrary any longer.

The next day, while Susan was shopping, I called her father and mother and asked their permission to marry their daughter. They both gave it gladly, though I think Susan's father, like all fathers, secretly thought no one would ever be good enough for his daughter. Her mother wept. I had never met them, though I'd talked to them on the phone several times since Susan moved in. I promised we would plan a trip to Miami to meet in person.

Susan came home soon after I hung up. I must have looked very ill, because she said, "Honey, are you alright? You don't look so good."

"I'm fine," I lied. I was scared to death. My hands were shaking. I grabbed my guitar that I hadn't played in years and said, "I'm going to get some new strings put on this. It might take awhile, since I don't know where the guitar store is."

I left the apartment and got in my truck, ready to endure one of the worst forms of torture I know of — the mall.

I was still shaky as I wandered through the mall. I saw a men's clothing store like the one I worked in when I was dating Penelope. I went inside and bought a new suit. I hadn't worn a suit since the Nixon administration. I was way out of my comfort zone.

After that, I wandered around the mall until I found a jewelry store. I bought a large diamond surrounded by smaller ones. The clerk put it in a mulberry-colored box. I wobbled out to my car and drove home, reminding myself to take deep breaths the whole way. In one day I'd broken many of my long-held beliefs. I'd given them up like sacrificial offerings for the woman I loved.

The next day I was nauseous and pale as a ghost. I kept disappearing into the bathroom. Susan thought I had a stomach virus. She suggested canceling our dinner date and doing it another night. I couldn't endure the thought of spending another day like this, so I convinced her I was well enough to go out.

We got in the car. Susan looked gorgeous in her full-length gray gown and red velvet waistcoat. Her beautiful blonde hair hung around her shoulders. "I've never seen you in a suit before. You look handsome and distinguished," she said, and suddenly I didn't mind wearing it.

Two blocks from the house I pulled into a florist and came back with two dozen red roses. Susan started crying.

We stopped at the Ritz-Carlton, a restaurant I knew Susan would love. The inside was dark, elegant, and filled with beautifully dressed people. Flowers in an Oriental vase adorned the entrance. The walls were rich mahogany wood. The food was exquisite—or so Susan said. I didn't notice. I mainly had bread and mineral water.

Susan couldn't help but notice my distress and fidgeting. Her face showed her concern. As we stood up to leave, she suggested we return home.

"No, the night is not over yet," I said. "We met by water, so now we need to spend time by water."

"What do you mean?" She looked confused, as if I had suggested a five-hour drive for a fast food dinner. After a few minutes of driving, I asked her to close her eyes. She obliged with a nervous smile.

"Keep them closed," I said, stopping the car. I helped her out and down a walkway, then said, "You can open your eyes now."

We stood in front of a handsome lake. A sculpted fountain sprayed water in a giant arc, casting dozens of rainbows. Ducks, geese, and swans swam on the shimmering water. We walked down a path that led to a gazebo by the water. We sat down just as the sun began to set. I could almost feel the turning of the earth. Susan was quiet beside me, soothed by the beauty and serenity around us.

I looked at Susan. "I want to ask you something."

"Your wish is my command. You've created the perfect evening."

I swallowed hard. I pretended that I dropped something on the ground and bent over to pick it up. I knelt down on one knee. "I've never done this before," I said in a faltering voice. Susan looked astounded.

"Susan, you are my best friend and my lover, and I want to spend the rest of my life with you. Will you marry me?"

I pulled the mulberry box from my coat pocket. She opened it and stared at the marquis diamond surrounded by smaller diamonds. I felt the lake, the geese, and the sun hold their breath. Then the look in her eyes reflected the radiance of the diamond, and the fear left me. "Of course I'll marry you."

She wrapped her arms around my neck, and we kissed and cried together. Susan was so overtaken by emotion, she was practically convulsing. At last she said, "I never expected you to ask so soon, especially after that whole waiting speech the other day. Of course I'll marry you, and love you for the rest of my life."

After more hugging, holding, and weeping, I told her I wanted to read her a couple of poems, just like our last morning together at Club Med. I read her a poem by a friend of mine, then I took out a folded piece of paper, a poem of my own, and read it in a hushed voice.

FAITH
I have stayed awake
all night,
hundreds of nights
trying to have just
enough faith to
fall asleep.

And there was a door
to marriage which
was always open.
I could have walked
through but I was
afraid, very afraid.

Then I met you.
I began sleeping.
I had a dream about Faith.
And this morning I
said to you, "Let's
go through this door together."

For Susan on July 13, 1997

Neither one of us could stop crying. I looked at the beautiful woman whom I loved more than anyone in the world, and said, "Thank you for the rest of my life."

We drove to our apartment and made love as if there were no forever. A couple of hours later I did another amazing thing—I called my parents and told them the news. My mother cried. My dad asked, "How much did you pay for the ring?" When I told him, he laughed and said I could have gotten a good used truck for that much money. "She might lose the ring or leave you, but a good truck lasts for years."

You have to be from Alabama to appreciate his logic.

CHAPTER 17
THE GREAT SABOTAGE GAME

"Desperado, why don't you come to your senses?
You've been out riding fences for so long now."
The Eagles

I spent the next few weeks discovering that a deeply intimate, loving relationship not only felt good, but also was terrifying. It left me completely vulnerable, a situation I'd managed to avoid up until now.

I was like General Custard's scout, one hand shielding my eyes from the sun, imagining I heard the thunder of countless horses over the hill. I couldn't stop thinking about all the things that could go wrong. Susan's old boyfriend could drive up in his gold Lexus and declare his undying love for her. Maybe she would decide she needed a younger man and head off in search of the Backstreet Boys. What if she suddenly decided she was gay? Or I was? Maybe Susan wasn't as perfect as she seemed; maybe she was like the character in Fatal Attraction—one minute sane and the next boiling bunnies.

One night I dreamed she and I were standing at a visitor's overlook in Yosemite, and she pushed me off. I woke up sweaty and ready to call the marriage off. I felt like I was going mad.

I talked out these horror stories with my therapist and friends. What if my career as a successful writer came to a screeching halt? How would I put our kid through college? What if I suddenly realized I had forgotten about a wife in a trailer park in Mississippi? My friends told me to take deep breaths, warm soothing baths, and a Xanax. I asked them if I was crazy. No, they said, most people feel such fears when they've made a big commitment. At least I wasn't crazy enough to tell Susan any of my Poe-like fantasies, and I swore my friends to secrecy.

But maybe I should have shared my fears with Susan. At least then she might have prepared herself for what happened next.

A month after getting engaged, Susan and I flew to Florida to introduce me to her family. The skies were a lush blue but I was in a fog. I wasn't thinking clearly at all. My emotions were tucked away in a safe place, a familiar place, somewhere I went every time someone wanted to be closer than I could handle, usually the same time things were becoming "too good to be true."

Contrary was back.

Contrary arrived at the Ft. Lauderdale Airport where he proceeded to destroy the very thing I held most dear, the love of a woman I had been searching and longing for all my life. While Susan and I started unpacking in our hotel room, Contrary, after checking to make sure my emotions were hidden safely, began sabotaging our relationship.

There are certain excuses that lovers have relied upon for centuries to end their relationships. Almost every goodbye uses at least one of them. You simply tell the person you love, who entrusted you with their heart, that either: a.) you need more time, b.) you need more space, c.) we're going way too fast, d.) there is someone else (even if there isn't), or e.) you have discovered a new sexual orientation. Any of these usually work.

I chose to combine several of the above to make my reasoning more convincing. I told Susan I needed more time and space, everything was going too fast, she was pushing too hard—and then I really twisted the knife.

"Susan, I'm too old for you. My God, when I was in love with Penelope in high school, you were an embryo. When you and I go out, people think you're my daughter."

This took several hours to say, mind you, but before the night was over, she was in tears. I struggled to comfort her as Contrary torpedoed any hopes of a future together. I said all the right things—"We'll be friends forever," "I think you're the most special person in the world," "This is the best thing in the long run," "You'll find someone closer to your own age and thank me ten years from now." Very disrespectful. I cannot believe I behaved so badly.

Susan cried. She was scared and very angry. Her body shook as I reasoned away our relationship. I turned that hotel room into a living hell for her. Finally, having reduced her to helpless sobbing, I called a cab to take her to her parent's house. We walked out to meet it. We kissed, and I held her limp body. The cab arrived. I opened the door and helped her get in.

"I'll fly back to Austin tomorrow," I said. "I won't expect you to come to the airport. I'll call you in a few days, after we've had some time to think."

"John, why are you doing this?" she asked, slumped and tiny in the back seat.

"It's for the best," I said. "I'm really sorry. Good night. I love you."

"I love you, too. Very, very much." Her voice was a mixture of disbelief and raw pain. As I closed the car door, she looked up at me, eyes full of tears, and said, "I can't believe it's over."

Chapter 18

AIRBORNE AGAIN

"To some extent, the young man, each time he leaves a woman, feels it as a victory, because he has escaped from his mother."
Robert Bly

Before I could leave the next morning, Susan came to the hotel. I opened the door, and she strode into the room, looking confident and collected.

"I'm not going to let your fear stand in the way of this relationship going further. We were meant to be together. Just because you have some issues to deal with doesn't mean we're over." She crossed her arms, her blue-green eyes glowing with determination. "You're not breaking up with me and that's that. Talk to a therapist, or whatever you need to do, get over your fears, and let's get on with it."

I was speechless, which is seldom true. Finally I said, "Okay." I had fought for love before, but I had never been fought for.

We held each other for a long time and wept from the rightness and courage of what she had done. I also cried out of fear. She was so determined to love me, I was afraid one day she would decide there was nothing there to love. Fifteen years earlier, Laurel, the woman I wrote about in my first book, *The Flying Boy*, wanted to love me despite my failings. I didn't let her. I hurt her until I drove her away, then wrote a book about why I acted the way I did.

I was determined not to fly this time.

I had been wrestling with depression on and off all my life, probably because I was raised during the Great Depression—my mother's. Depression ran in the family, including my father, sister, aunts, uncles, and cousins. Much of mine was biochemical and improved by serotonin-enhancing drugs, but during this difficult time in my relationship with Susan, medication alone was not enough. I needed intense therapy.

I returned to Austin more than a little frightened, but somewhat ecstatic that a woman as beautiful and strong as Susan really wanted to love me. When I got home I called my therapist, Dr. Maynard, and scheduled an appointment, determined to fix the part of me that wanted to fly. I wanted to be with Susan, and that meant changing my life.

Dr. Maynard suggested I might be suffering from anaclitic depression. "What the hell is that?" I asked, mildly disturbed because I thought I had read everything out there on depression. I had never heard of it, and neither had anyone else apparently, since I couldn't find it in any textbooks or self-help books, nor had a therapist ever mentioned it. Volumes have been written on biochemical depression, but almost nothing on anaclitic depression.

"Anaclitic depression is a Freudian idea that a person suffers deeply from never having received non-libidinous love."

"What the hell is non-libidinous love?"

Dr. Maynard explained that when a child comes into the world, he or she should be the center of the universe. A child is supposed to be loved without any trace of sexual energy attached to that love.

I was getting scared. "You're not talking about incest are you?"

"No," he said quickly. "In most dysfunctional families, either the mother, the father, or another child is the center of the universe. Let's say a woman's husband was emotionally absent, she might turn to a son or daughter for the comfort, support, and attention that the husband doesn't provide. A type of non-malicious, non-sexual love develops between the mother and the child."

I listened and started weeping. He just described what my mother had done to me all during my childhood, adolescence, and early adulthood. Dr. Maynard suggested I read Dr. Pat Love's book called *The Emotional Incest Syndrome* and Alice Miller's *The Drama of the Gifted Child*.

I went home and read both books. In Love's book, she explains that sometimes a needy mother or father — completely unintentionally — uses a son or daughter as a surrogate husband, wife, confidant, counselor, or savior. The book elucidated why I could relate to clients of mine who had been victims of incest or sexually molested. Even though there was no physical violation with my mother and me, psychosexual incest took place.

In Miller's groundbreaking book, she proposes the idea that when children look into their mothers' eyes, they are supposed to see her love for them radiating back. Many children, like me, saw darkness, emptiness, and hunger. I fed my mother's hunger for love, something her parents and my father were unable to provide.

Being emotional food for a father or mother creates distrust, disillusionment and disastrous relationships. It always destroys a child's self-esteem, since their acceptance as a person becomes conditional. Their value is determined by what they can give to the parent, instead of being inherent. Adults who suffer from Anaclitic depression usually cover it up with alcoholism, workaholism, sexual addiction, and other addictions and behaviors.

During another therapy session, Dr. Maynard explained that if a child never experienced a "pure" love, one with no sexual connection, he or she would often be a victim of Anaclitic depression. Bruehl and Bethelard explain it in their book, *Cherishment: A Psychology of the Heart*, by saying that Anaclitic depression results from a love "that involves literally leaning on, touching on, being dependent on a person." In many ways, this describes what my mother did to me, and I learned that same dependence, needing women to comfort and nurture me the same way I had done for my mother.

When faced with a healthy love, such as what Susan now offered, I descended into a deep depression, since it only reminded me of what I had never experienced.

Over the next several months, under Dr. Maynard's care, I discovered the cure is in the descent. The more I let Susan love me, the more I felt the long-buried grief and anger for having never received unconditional love. I also grew more confident of the reality and dependability of Susan's love. Experiencing these emotions was the key to my healing.

I came to understand the work of Takio Doi, Japan's most famous psychiatrist. He states that in Japan there is an expectation of being cherished, not only in childhood, but also for life. According to Doi, the word for this expectation to be cherished is *amae*, which means "an emotion that is constituted tacitly. It is telepathic, pre-linguistic, and does not need the medium of language. It is communicated directly from heart to heart." In short, it means spontaneous affection. In our language, the closest word to it is cherishment. So *amae*, or to cherish, means: "make me pleasurably safe, make me strong! Tend this green shoot! The expectation is not sexual." (Bruehl and Bethelard)

Like everyone else, I came into the world hungry and thirsty. When ample food (love and nurturing) was not forthcoming, I began to believe I didn't deserve it. As Doi says in his book, *An Anatomy of Dependence*, it is a child's birthright to feel he or she is cherished without having to do anything, give anything, or be anything."

With *amae*, or cherishment, a kind of receptivity to being loved is born. I was unable to receive healthy love because I had never felt truly cherished, nor did I expect to be. After all, I hadn't had much practice.

I wrote a poem for Susan, attempting to explain my difficulty in receiving her love.

TWO KINDS OF LOVE
Last night you looked so lovingly at
me
I had to turn away.
You know there are two ways to
love,
A friend said to me — face to face,
Eye to eye, skin to skin — whole-
heartedly.

And in the other way one gives love
At a distance and hopes they pick
up the clues.

Yesterday I bought you a dozen red
roses,

Each one was a clue and a promise
That some day I would learn to love
the
Open way of the flower.

While Susan was no saint, she was capable of offering the kind of love I needed in order to heal. All I had to do was let her nature take its course. It was not easy. I knew more about leaving and flying than staying and being loved. Her love was like a magnet, drawing out the steel rod stuck in my heart since childhood. The more she loved me, the more it hurt, the more it hurt the deeper I went into the depression I had been avoiding all my life.

Between Dr. Maynard's wisdom and support and Susan's love and nurturing, I finally came out of denial and admitted my problems with depression and commitment. And more importantly, I finally discovered there was a cure: learning to receive love. If I could do that, I had a chance.

CHAPTER 19
RETURN TO COURTING

"And now, for the rest of the story."
Paul Harvey

Of course there was more to my attempted sabotage than anaclitic depression. I harbored many different fears that turned me into a human wrecking ball. They say that when an adult who was born blind suddenly gains their sight later in life, whether through surgery or some other miracle, they are terrified by what they see, even though they only see the scenes of everyday life we take for granted. It takes a long time for them to adjust to having vision. When I met Susan, I discovered a new, colorful life filled with love and intimacy. She trusted me with her soul, the most tender and intimate place inside of her, and the sight of it frightened me. People would say to me, "Man, she is gorgeous!" and I would say, "Oh, you think so? She's even more beautiful on the inside." I had never, except for Penelope, seen the soul of a woman. I avoided knowing other women so intimately. It's one thing to leave or be left by a lover; you can recover relatively quickly and move on to the next one. But a best friend who is also your lover, who does not hesitate to show you her soul and who is willing to love you like you've never been loved, to lose that is devastating. Penelope proved that years before.

I have asked three women to marry me, but in each case it was after Contrary had wrecked the relationship. My marriage proposals were futile attempts to avoid dealing with the agony of separation and loss, and served as some weird kind of rationalization I could pull out when other women asked why I hadn't been married before. I could always say, "I asked."

Bill and I were driving in the country one day, and he said, "Why didn't you ask Grace [the last woman I lived with] to marry you?"

"I think I must be terrified of marriage," I said. "You know one out of two marriages end in divorce. Half my aunts and uncles have divorced over the last twenty-five years."

"John, I don't think you're afraid of marriage half as much as you're afraid of divorce."

Bill was right, as usual. Alimony, custody battles, and community property had lain to waste many a good man, woman and child. I was proud of the fact that unlike so many of my friends and peers, I was halfway through life without having gone through a divorce. I lived with women whenever I could for as long as I could, and then no mess, no attorneys, just move out.

But nothing would be simple or painless about losing Susan.

After our argument in Miami, Susan moved out of Austin and found her dream apartment in Atlanta. Like me, she had a job that allowed her to work from anywhere. We continued to work on our relationship, but our engagement was on a trial basis, and after the stunt I pulled, I expected no less.

I kept my apartment in Austin and visited her in Atlanta when I wasn't on the road lecturing. I traveled through the Atlanta airport all the time, so for Susan to get an apartment there was perfect. I thought we would have a better chance of making amends in a neutral city where ghosts wouldn't be lurking around every corner.

I wanted to see and court the soul of the woman I loved, without feeling threatened or afraid. I wanted to offer her the kind of love she deserved.

I made a list of things I had to do if Susan and I were to develop a healthy relationship:

1. I would have to let go of as many expectations as possible, since an expectation is a premeditated resentment.

2. I had to stop performing the part of a lover, and instead learn to give and receive love.

3. I would create a new twelve-step program for recovering control addicts.

4. I would give up my lifelong desire for perfection in both myself and the one I loved.

5.   I would actively court Susan's soul, and not just talk about it.

I took the time to learn how Susan "read" love. One of the main ways she felt and received love was through her delicate, yet strong, body. Touch told her everything she needed to know, and not only sexual touch, but the gentle touch of an arm stroked, a hand held, a shoulder massaged, her face gently caressed. All told her how deeply she was cared for. This did not come naturally to me, so I had to consciously work on it. After all, the goal was not for me to do what felt most comfortable, but to make Susan feel loved.

Another way I expressed my love for Susan was to avoid looking at other women's bodies. With earlier lovers, I had used the typical rationales: "I'm just looking, not touching;" "Window shopping, not buying;" or, "At least I'm looking at her while I'm with you, baby, instead of behind your back." Those were all poor excuses for disrespecting a woman. Thank God I had an older, wiser man teach me that all women thrive on respect.

One day during our trial engagement, Susan stopped me in front of a bookstore, hugged my arm, and said, "I just want to thank you."

"What for, sweetie?" I said.

"I've never seen you ogle or even glance at another woman when we're out in public. I just want you to know how much I appreciate that. Every man I've dated looked at other women when we were out together. It made me feel cheap."

I have to say that I was grateful for what she said, but sad at the same time. The faces of several wonderful women flashed before my eyes, women that should have known the same respect.

Susan was more open with me when I maintained eye contact during conversations. It let her know I was really listening, and not trying to sneak a peek at the newspaper or television. I did other things for her as well. I never questioned her fidelity. I never regarded cleaning or cooking as women's work, but tried my best to tackle half of the household responsibilities. These things may not seem like much, but they are how love is expressed in daily life, and Susan appreciated them.

The ways of courting a woman's soul are numberless, and many of them are as unique as each woman. Maybe the single best thing I learned was not to take anything for granted—above all, the woman I love. The best way to court a woman's soul is to never stop courting her.

Our trial period went well. Finally we were ready for a wedding to end all weddings. Come be our guests.

CHAPTER 20

THE FLYING BOY COMES TO EARTH

"Have you ever really, really ever loved a woman?"
Bryan Adams

The Sallie Howard Memorial Chapel was the perfect setting for our wedding. It's a small stone church constructed around a huge boulder on a hillside in the Alabama mountains. Colonel Milford designed and built the church in honor of his wife after she passed away. The chapel was completed in 1937, and even all these years later, Colonel Milford's love for his wife is tangible to everyone who visits.

We reserved the chapel and a minister, but a few weeks later discovered my best man, Robert Bly, couldn't make the date we set. It was very important to me that he be there, so we advanced the date to accommodate him. With the wedding now only four months away, we shifted into maximum overdrive. We still had to find our wedding clothes, register, order and send invitations, and deal with a million other details.

Susan chose to wear a beautiful antique gown from 1915, my favorite historical period. I knew I'd feel uncomfortable wearing modern formal wear, so I visited a used clothing store. They had a turn-

of-the-century wedding frock coat that almost fit —
if I lost a hundred pounds and shrank to four feet
tall. But I did find some spats from the 1920's that
I asked them to hold.

A few weeks later, when I went back to buy the
spats, the owner hustled out of the storeroom, saying, "I'm so glad you came back. We wanted to call
you, but you didn't leave your number." She held
up an 1885 morning coat. It was in mint condition
and fit my body as if tailor-made.

The wedding was planned as the culminating
event of a long weekend in the country. Close
friends arrived on Friday. We built a huge bonfire
and brought out guitars and singing voices that
drove the locals crazy. As the fire crackled, we ate
and drank and danced and told stories and toasted
everybody. There was so much laughter that I
cried a couple of times, unable to hold so much
emotion inside.

On Saturday we all gathered in the woods
beside my cottage. Small shrines and places to
worship and meditate were scattered among the
trees. Our friends are as beautifully diverse as the
wildflowers that grow on Mentone Mountain. We
all formed a circle for the first wedding ceremony.
Martíne Prechtel, a friend trained as a ritual leader
in his Guatemalan village and chief of 40,000,
draped Susan and me in a hand woven blue and
yellow blanket. He said we were to sleep under it
for a year. Then he held out a bowl I'd owned for
fifteen years; it was the only household object

remaining from the first woman I'd ever lived with, Laurel. I looked at the bowl and thought of Penelope, Trisha, and all the other women I'd loved; I thought of the years I'd spent running from intimacy, and of how I'd almost robbed Susan and myself of this moment. I threw the bowl hard against the ground. Susan and I stomped on it until it disintegrated into dozens of pieces.

The marriage on Sunday felt like a fairy tale. Marlene, Susan's matron of honor, had decorated the church as brightly as the White House Christmas tree. When Susan floated down the aisle and I caught sight of her radiance, I almost fainted. I felt Robert's hand take my arm and straighten me back up.

The minister, Marty Newman, was a young woman I'd known for years. At the start of the ceremony she made a slip of the tongue, saying, "We are all gathered here today to marry God to this young woman." There were a few gasps and a bit of laughter, but everyone accepted the mistake in good humor.

Several people were involved with the ceremony. Susan's aunt played "I Love Thee Truly" on the harp, then other musicians played Spanish guitars like wild, joyful gypsies.

Robert read the same poem of his that I read to Susan on the island, "The Third Body."

A man and a woman sit near each
other, and they do not long
at this moment to be older, or
younger, nor born
in any other nation, or time, or
place.
They are content to be where they
are, talking or not-talking.
Their breaths together feed someone
whom we do not know.
The man sees the way her fingers
move;
he sees her hands close around a
book she hands to him.
They obey a third body that they
share in common.
They have made a promise to love
that body.
Age may come, parting may come,
death will come.
A man and a woman sit near each
other;
as they breathe they feed someone
we do not know,
someone we know of, whom we
have never seen.

Robert read another poem. Part of it goes:

When men and women come
together,

how much they have to abandon!
Wrens
make their nests of fancy threads
and string ends, animals
abandon all their money each year.
What is it that men and women
leave?
Harder than wrens' doing, they
have
to abandon their longing for the
perfect.

The inner nest not made by instinct
will never be quite round,
and each has to enter the nest
made by the other imperfect bird.

While he read, I looked at the people who had gathered to support Susan and me. My parents were there, even though I had seen them only once in ten years. My mother's eyes were filled with tears; it felt good to see her happy. Susan's parents, Bill and Otilia Hasewinkle, were dressed like living rainbows, and both of them were crying. My aunt and sister were present as well, as was my brother, who looked like me twenty years earlier. My old friends from high school, Bob and Jana, Dane and Tracey, Roger and Carolyn, were there (they thought I'd never get married). Bill Stott, my other best man, stood by me with a sweet and goofy smile on his face.

Susan and I stood in the shadow of the chapel's mammoth rock and spoke our vows beneath the huge beam that spans the entire width of the church. On it is painted, "God has always been as good to me as I would let him be."

EPILOGUE

Susan and I have been married six years. Has it all been heaven? No. There have been arguments, misunderstandings, and disappointments. There have been money problems and a miscarriage--but we're still hopeful. More important than all that, we are happy. I have never been as happy and alive as I am now. I believe Susan means it when she says the same. For the first time in my life, I'm relaxed; I don't have to fight to be myself or to impress others. Thanks to Susan's support and understanding—her love—I can sit back and let life come to me, and meet it the way I choose.

And Susan? Well, you'd have to ask her. I do know she loves her work, which calls upon her genius at connecting with people. She also enjoys graphic design (she designed this book cover to cover). Sometimes I worry she doesn't have enough time to exercise those talents, but she says she's living as she wants to, and that makes me happy. I bet there are few couples who cuddle as much or as long as we do.

There are six final ideas that I'd like to share with you.

First, to have a healthy long-term relationship, you need to deal with your past. You can't make a healthy, free choice about your soulmate so long as you're making decisions based on the opinions and actions of people in your past (even rebellion is a form of control). You can't be alive in the present moment if you're carting around needs or hurts created by people in your past. To use a metaphor, you can't be happy dancing with a partner unless you can first be happy dancing alone.

Second, to find a long-term relationship, you have to be looking for one, which means you can't be screwing around. As a couple, Susan and I work well because we were mature enough to make a commitment. I had already sown my wild oats before I met Susan, so I no longer had the need to appease my penis any more. Some men, and some women, never get to this stage. It's better for everyone if they acknowledge this and not marry.

Third, you need to know what you're looking for. You can't search for a partner by waiting to see what comes your way. You need to analyze yourself and your romantic history to discover what your needs and wishes are. You may need to draw up a list, as I did.

Fourth, take your time courting to find whether or not the person you're with can supply what you're looking for. My grandfather courted my grandmother a long time. He walked to church with her, took her to movies, and sat and talked on the front porch swing many hours before they even kissed. Compatibility can only be judged over time; it involves a lot of talking and objectiveness. If your prospective partner has different aspirations, intellectual concerns, or religious preferences to yours, then raise a red flag. If her idea of a good time is shopping in the mall and you hate the mall, what are you going to do together on the weekend? Do you have similar opinions about family? Finances? Can you accommodate your differences?

Ask questions and listen to the answers. If you can't make the time or find the courage to talk to this person, then either it's a bad relationship or you aren't ready to make a commitment. Communication is the key for a healthy relationship. For men, don't fear that asking all your questions and talking so much will alienate a woman. On the contrary, it will make her feel respected and loved. If it doesn't, then she isn't the woman for you.

Fifth, once you've taken the time to know her, begin — gently, sensitively — experimenting. She says she shares your love of hiking; try her on an easy hour's walk along the river. She says she enjoys watching pro football on TV; see how she puts up with a month of Sundays. Or, if she likes touching, try different kinds of touching — a body massage, shampooing her hair, kissing the backs of her legs. Find ways to touch her without becoming sexual.

Sixth, and sometimes most difficult, let him or her learn more about you. In order for them to really love and accept you, they have to know you, warts and all. If they don't like warts, then you won't be happy in the relationship because you won't feel accepted. Be honest about your hopes, fears, ambitions, and preferences. Welcome the probing questions. Ladies, if he has no curiosity about you, then he is indifferent and doesn't really love you.

Most importantly, take the time to do these things now, so you don't regret your decisions down the road, and so you can find true joy with the person you love.

Thanks for having read my book. Susan and I wish you all possible luck in finding a healthy and loving relationship, and now we retreat from public exposure of our relationship into its private enjoyment.

ACKNOWLEDGEMENTS

I would like to thank: A woman named Susan who shines like the Sun and the Moon and the Stars. Bill Stott, who has loved me for over twenty years. His generous editing has amounted to collaboration, and, if he'd let me, I'd put his name on the title page with mine. Robert Bly, who has been a dear friend and teacher. He has taught me about love, life, and everything in between, and has edited this work and many others.

This book is so much more than it would have been thanks to Jennifer Hanawalt, Senior Editor of Mandala Publishing, who painstakingly edited this book and made invaluable comments and suggestions.

Special thanks go to Kim and Julie Lillie, loving friends who supported this project emotionally, spiritually and financially.

Some people's contributions are so significant they can be compared to a mountain, a thunderstorm, an ocean in their importance. Then there are people whose help is like a child's smile or a fine mist falling on silent, southern forests--subtle, but equally important. Here are just a few: Karen Blicher, Vijay Director, Connie Burns, Fran DeFlorio, Phyllis Rice, Bob and Jana White, Roger and Carolyn Fuller, Dane Dixon, Dan Jones, Patrick Kane, Pam Mauch, all my workshop participants, clients, producers, my 12-Step friends, Mio, Casper, and Lucy. I love you all and may God bless you.

In Memoriam

JIMMY HENDERSON

A brother and friend

OTHER WORKS BY JOHN LEE

Books

The Flying Boy: Healing the Wounded Man
The Flying Boy II: The Journey Continues
The Flying Boy III: Stepping Into the Mystery
At My Father's Wedding: Reclaiming Our True Masculinity
Facing the Fire: Experiencing and Expressing Anger Appropriately
Writing From The Body: For Writers, Artists, and Dreamers Who
   Long To Free Their Voice
Sleeping In Public (a book of poems)*
Growing Yourself Back Up
Recovery: Plain and Simple*

Audiotapes

Why Men Can't Feel and The Price Women Pay*
Saying Goodbye to Mom and Dad*
Grieving: A Key to Healing*
Expressing Your Anger Appropriately*
Healing the Father-Son Wound*
The Rhythm of Closeness*
Men in Balance*
How to Love Someone and Not Lose Yourself*
Growing Yourself Back Up*
The Flying Boy*
At My Father's Wedding*
On the Mountain of Tears and Laughter* (poetry reading with
   Robert Bly)
Sleeping In Public*

Video

Being Who You Are: Creating an Artful Life*

*Available only at *www.jlcsonline.com*

To order books and tapes and view John Lee's event schedule,
please visit
www.jlcsonline.com or contact John Lee at:

JL Creative Services, Inc.
PO Box 769
Woodstock, GA 30188
Tel: 678-494-1296
info@jlcsonline.com